First published 2010 by
Aurum Press Limited
7 Greenland Street
London NW1 0ND
www.aurumpress.co.uk

A catalogue record for this book is available from the British Library.

ISBN 978 1 84513 590 4

10 9 8 7 6 5 4 3 2
2015 2014 2013 2012 2011 2010

Text design and typesetting by Blue Gum
Illustrations by Richard Beacham

Printed and bound in Great Britain by the
MPG Books Group, Bodmin, Cornwall

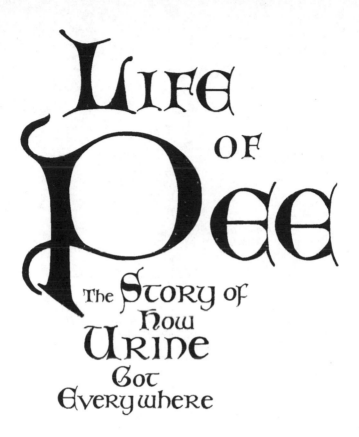

LIFE OF PEE

OF

THE STORY OF HOW URINE GOT EVERYWHERE

SALLY MAGNUSSON

Contents

Introduction

THERE WAS A TIME when the faint but unmistakeable whiff of wool mixed with human urine was almost as familiar in the august corridors of Britain's House of Lords as pipe-smoke.

Thankfully, this had nothing to do with aristocratic incontinence: their lordships may have been getting on a bit, but in this matter they were blameless. It wasn't even that sort of smell. Nostalgic weavers claim the fragrance that clung to the checked plaids beloved of peers was actually rather pleasant. 'Lovely' is how they remember the designer smell of Harris Tweed.

The people of Harris may not be hugely flattered to hear it was their skill with stale pee that inspired this book, but I found the story spell-binding. What an astonishing thing, this strange alchemy that could conjure from dirty fleeces and old household pee something as sweet to the nose and ravishingly beautiful to the eye as handmade tweed. How wonderful that in the teeming pee-tubs of Harris – second from the top in the necklace of jewels we call the Outer Hebrides – a tradition which sustained entire economies across Europe for hundreds of years should have been flourishing far into the twentieth century.

And how, well, humbling, that this unremarked substance we are always so desperate to get rid of should turn out to have led a heroic undercover life as one of the most versatile industrial agents on earth.

On Harris I learned that every stage of the cottage tweed industry depended on urine. It fixed and in some cases released the dyes, scoured away the grease and finally shrank the cloth during the time-honoured 'waulking' – a process to which every Walker in the phone-book (not to mention Mr and Mrs Fuller and Tucker) owes his or her name. One renowned island weaver was still summoning full chamber pots from her neighbours until shortly before her death in 1996. But if Harris Tweed is what first set me wondering, I might only have tinkered at the edges of curiosity had it not been for the man at the party.

A stranger suddenly confided over a glass of wine that he had cancer and was treating it by drinking his own urine. Too serious to laugh, too bizarre to keep a straight face, it was a situation for which party-talk convention hardly prepares you. I think, to my shame, I might have let slip a giggle. Yet the young man maintained with some dignity that urine therapy was a credible treatment showing, thus far, signs of success. I wished him well and reflected on the way home that soaking tweeds in domestic pee had nothing on this.

There was one more unexpected encounter with urine, another intimation of a mysterious double-life, that finally propelled me into investigating. This time I was having a back massage. After thumping me around for a while in the usual manner the masseuse advised, *sotto voce*, that actually I would get the swiftest possible relief by soaking a cloth in pee and keeping it pressed into my lower back all night. She often did it herself. Eased the muscles wonderfully, she whispered.

That evening I toyed with the advice just long enough to work out there was no way I could spend the night bound round with a sodden cloth of decomposing urine without attracting the attention of my husband, who is just the sort of chap to mention it to the postman next morning. But at that point I did start to look into it. What else was this stuff getting up to behind, as it were, all our backs?

. . .

This is not something you may feel inclined to check, but urine doesn't smell. Not at first anyway. It emerges into the world clean as a baby and virtually odour-less. A by-product of the blood, it consists of 95% water and 5% bio-chemicals the body is anxious to expel because they are excess to requirements or toxic.

Blood chugs around the body like an endlessly circulating train. On board are food molecules and other nutrients, as well as the red and white blood cells, plasma, antibodies, proteins, hormones and enzymes manufactured in different parts of the body. On its way it passes through the chemical processing factory of the liver, where nutrients from food and drink are converted into forms the body's cells can use. Toxins like ammonia are disarmed here and microbes destroyed.

Then the blood (a quarter of our entire supply every minute) trundles on to the kidneys, to be processed by tiny units called nephrons which filter out water, salts, acids, alkalis and the nitrogen-containing compounds like urea that are produced from the breakdown of proteins. In the form of urine they pass out of the kidneys, into the bladder, and away. In 24 hours a pair of adult kidneys will filter around 150 litres of blood and produce about 1.5 litres of urine.

Thus our hero emerges into a world that steadfastly looks the other way. Which is hardly surprising. Urine does keep unpleasant company. While nutrients pass through the small intestine into the blood, indigestible food heads off separately into the large intestine. Along with some excess water, cells and bacteria, it is eventually expelled as faeces (from the Latin *faex*, or dregs), a seriously mucky substance that has rather brought the neighbourhood into disrepute.

Urine, on the other hand, arrives on the scene pristine clean and bouncing with some of the most vital, life-sustaining chemicals on earth, like nitrogen and potassium. Excreted pharmaceuticals will be in there as well, of course, as well as literally thousands of other chemical compounds. A list of the more familiar ones might include:

- ❖ Adrenaline, Ammonium, Ascorbic acid, Allantoin, Amino acids
- ❖ Bicarbonate, Biotin
- ❖ Calcium, Chloride, Creatinine
- ❖ Dopamine
- ❖ Folic acid
- ❖ Glucose
- ❖ Inositol, Iodine, Iron
- ❖ Magnesium, Manganese
- ❖ Nitrogen
- ❖ Ornithine

* Pantothenic acid, Phosphorus, Potassium, Proteins
* Riboflavin
* Sodium, Sulphur
* Urea, Uric acid
* Vitamins
* Zinc

Of course, the state of sterile, odour-free bliss in which urine first encounters the world doesn't last long. Ammonia is rattling its cage. As a poison (one of the compounds of waste nitrogen left over from the process of breaking down proteins), ammonia is dangerous. But the body is deft at protecting itself, and the liver solves the problem by storing the ammonia in urea, a more complex, water-soluble compound, until it can be safely smuggled out in urine. In fact, even after leaving the body, ammonia remains neutralised. It stays locked up and harmless until exposed to everyday bacteria in the air, soil, under the toilet seat, or on any infected part of our body on its way out. Only then is the urea converted back into ammonia.

As Joseph Lister discovered in the experiments that led to his discovery of antisepsis, urine could remain more or less sterile for years if protected from microbes in the air. The Young Ones in the anarchic 1980s sitcom hit on the same principle by keeping a urine sample fresh in the fridge at a temperature too low for bacteria to function properly.

This, then, is the biological journey that has made urine so extraordinarily versatile: able to perform a sterile medical function one day, make bread rise or ale foam the next and adopt a dazzling new role as a toxic detergent and dye-fixer the day after that. It's where urine acquired the tools to change the world.

. . .

Less squeamish generations than ours took the productivity of pee for granted. Like plants, animals, minerals, water and the bounty of the sea, urine was regarded as a natural resource, copiously available and self-evidently capable of being put to work. Long before anyone knew it contained the bio-chemicals that created the planet and continue to sustain its life, people understood that urine was powerful.

So, from the earliest days of history we find it being examined for illness, tested for pregnancy, recycled for health, spread on fields and used to clean just about anything. We find the Romans basing their commercial laundry system on it (one of their emperors even had the *chutzpah* to tax it) and the medieval mind embracing it as the key to the secrets of the universe itself.

We discover it making dyes, strengthening swords, painting stained glass and decorating manuscripts. It was the resource that supported Europe's woollen industry for hundreds of years, provided gunpowder for sundry wars and kept Britain in alum until the 1870s. Bought and sold, traded and transported, even carried to work in jugs, it was in such demand in the seventeenth century that the peeing populace could barely keep up.

In time alchemists seeking gold in it gave way to the discoveries of real chemists. The founder of modern dentistry recommended it as a mouthwash and doctors learned how to treat disease with its components. By the time soldiers faced killer gas in the trenches of Ypres, they knew enough to use it as a makeshift gas mask.

In the modern world, where urine has difficulty living down its image as something not altogether 'nice', its other life is conducted less brazenly than of old. All the same, a growing scientific understanding of how it operates has driven its career in new directions. People are making meals from it in space, producing vehicle fuel, forging mud-bricks. It's on the frontline of a high-stakes battle for the soul of sport. Businesses are raking in profits from harvested hormones. Women unwittingly rely on it to treat infertility and the menopause.

Urine even manages to behave badly in more ways than we might dream. We find it humiliating enemies, spreading typhoid, forging coins, contaminating perfume, punishing witches and claiming responsibility for a stoned Santa Claus. In art, song and literature (where its reputation robbed *The Waste Land* of a crucial couplet), it engenders boisterous controversy.

More serious is the spectre of pollution. Urine surges into the waterways of the world with all our medical secrets and illegal vices still on board. Into our rivers it dumps minute traces of every drug we consume, from chemo to cocaine, for fish to imbibe and quite possibly some of us to meet again in our taps. Our urine footprint, it turns out, is as indelible as our carbon one.

And we do produce an awful lot of it. In a single year humans alone make almost enough to replace the entire contents of Loch Lomond. It would take a million Olympic-sized swimming pools to store it all. Add the incalculable volume contributed by the animals of the world and we could probably displace a small ocean.

So are we, by any chance, missing a trick by allowing urine to remain so coyly undercover? When you realise that by recycling farmyard urine into the manufacture of plastics some bold companies are improving air quality, saving fossil fuels and reducing the financial and energy costs of transporting synthetically produced urea, you do start to ask how much our ignorance about the potential of pee might be costing the planet.

Is it entirely wise, you begin to wonder, to waste as much water as we do flushing it away, when it then has to be expensively treated to remove the nitrogen that we then get from somewhere else to manufacture fertiliser? Is it not strange to go to the trouble we do to recycle glass bottles but not, say, globally depleted phosphorus? Once you start asking the questions, our arms-length, nose-pinched attitude to urine begins to look almost culpably short-sighted.

I never did meet the nameless man from the party again to find out how his story ended. I wish I knew. Nor can I vouch for the multifarious other medical claims made for urine on the outer reaches of the alternative health movement. What I have certainly concluded, though, is that in a world that has trampled blithely across almost every other taboo, a dispassionate and steady-eyed reassessment of the forgotten life of pee is urgently overdue.

Words to the Wise

SINCE LANGUAGE IS AN important feature of the life of our subject, you may find it helpful to have a frame of reference. Although this list makes no claim to be exhaustive, the vocabulary is as joyously varied and tortuously nuanced as any in the English language. Some words have died with the role they once played and others we can only hope will whizz off very soon, but every one of them is a footprint in a well-travelled life.

URINE

Oh dear, *urine*. Such a prissy word. An ugly, clomping thing which was borrowed into English via Old French from the Latin *urina* and Greek *ouron*, at a time when medieval physicians needed a solid utilitarian expression for the substance they were examining in their glass flasks to diagnose illness. Its first recorded usage was around 1325 ('*He wol wagge his urine in a vessel of glaz*'), since which time it has remained the staid maiden aunt of the many upstarts that English has evolved to rival it. Doctors, scientists and authors nearer home who want to sound matter-of-fact and inoffensive choose *urine*. It's safe, formal, a little prim. So boring, in fact, that it took centuries even to summon up the energy to engender a verb: the sedate *urinate* first popped up in a medical textbook as late as 1599. No-one will be surprised that when the art of medieval uroscopy degenerated into quackery, detractors turned to a word with a bit of oomph to express their contempt[*].

LANT

Lant is the tough, muscular native word that English passed up in favour of *urine*. In its original form, *hland*, it appears in Old English writings from around 1000. Exactly the same word in Old Norse strode confidently on into modern Icelandic, but in England *hland* became *lant* and then more or less disappeared – except in the

---

See: Pisse-Prophets[*]

north-west, where it stayed to denote the stale urine used as an industrial agent. *Lant* was associated with cleaning floors, flavouring ale (for which it bred its own verb, *leint*)*, glazing pastries, scouring clothes, pickling copper and making dyes.

In Elizabethan England the much-married Bess of Hardwick, a Lady of the Bedchamber at court with a family pile in Derbyshire, owned a silver *lant* pot and comb for hairdressing. Since she sported the same fashionably red hair as her friend Queen Elizabeth, we might assume she perfected the tint with the help of the urine in that silver pot, since *lant* was an agent in making all sorts of dyes. In the late 1880s we find it being mixed with lime to ward off birds from newly sown wheat.[1]

Just before he died at the age of 96, the former union leader Jack Jones described hearing the shout of 'Lant!' each morning as a boy growing up in Garston, Liverpool. A lad would be trundling a metal barrel on wheels round the streets, collecting the *lant* for use in the pickling process in the nearby copper works, where the metal was immersed in urine to remove scaling. 'The women would go out and empty the contents of their chamber-pots into the barrel,' said Mr Jones, who died in April 2009.

When it was no longer used for these purposes, the word itself began to ail in the north-west of England and is now rarely heard.

WASH

In Scotland and parts of northern England another taut Old English word, *wæsc* (which became *wesche* and then *wash*), was used in the same way as *lant* to denote stale urine used as a detergent or mordant. Doubtless the help it supplied in washing clothes supplied the link. Satirising the pompous prescriptions of apothecaries in *Sum Practysis of Medecyne*, the fifteenth-century Scottish poet Robert Henryson offers a remedy for sleeplessness that includes 'reid nettill seid in strang wesche to steip, / For to bath your ba cod' (red nettles steeped in stale urine for bathing your scrotum).

See: 𝕭eer*

WEETING

In Yorkshire *weeting* was used as an alternative to *wash*. Required in prodigious quantities to service the woollen industry around Huddersfield, *weeting* was collected from the villages each day by horse and cart, like a milk-round in reverse. The draught-horse (or *dobbin*) was gloriously dubbed the *weetin-dob*[*].

CHAMBER-LYE

Another word reflecting urine's former glory as a *lye*, or detergent. The uses of *chamber-lye* included medical remedies ('Take chamberly, and salte, and seeth them together, and washe the places where the skinne is cut of'[2]), adulterating beer (a 1743 brewer's manual complains of 'that nasty, horrid, and detestable piece of cunning and knavery … of putting chamberlye, or human urine, into their pale or amber two-penny malt drink')[**], and making gunpowder from the *chamber-lye* patriotically supplied by Southern ladies in the American Civil War[***].

PISS

It barged into English with the Normans and behaved so badly that *piss* is now beyond the pale of polite usage and relegated in dictionaries to 'coarse slang'. Both noun and verb are rumbustiously derived from the sound of a bladder emptying – a derivation English shares with a number of Romance languages (Anglo-Norman *pisser*, Old French *pissier*, Old Occitan *pissar*, Catalan *pixar*, Italian *pisciare* and so on). To this day people are still merrily *pissing*, in one spelling or another, from Scandinavia to Italy. Associated from the first with stench and chamber-pots, over-indulgence and riotous behaviour, the word has always lived colourfully. It was soon breeding the kind of rowdy metaphors that are well below the dignity of the *urine* brand. Thus we have:

See: Fullers, Tuckers and Walkers[*]
    Beer[**]
    Confederate Belles[***]

- ❖ **Piss away:** to squander or waste.
- ❖ **Piss one's tallow:** to lose fat (like bucks growing lean after rutting-time).
- ❖ **Piss through the same quill:** to agree or be of one accord.
- ❖ **Piss against (or in) the wind:** to act ineffectually or waste your time (originally employed in the graphic proverb 'He who pisses against the wind, wets his shirt').
- ❖ **Piss on someone's parade or (curiously) their chips:** to spoil plans.
- ❖ **Piss up a rope:** to do something pointless.
- ❖ **Piss in a pocket:** to flatter or seek to ingratiate.
- ❖ **Piss about:** to waste time.
- ❖ **Piss off:** to leave or go away.
- ❖ **Piss someone off:** to annoy or irritate.
- ❖ **Piss on:** to show contempt or scorn toward.
- ❖ **Piss up:** to ruin, make a mess of.
- ❖ **Piss and wind:** empty talk or bombast.
- ❖ **Piss and vinegar:** energy or youthful aggression.
- ❖ **Take the piss:** to make fun of someone, mock or deride.
- ❖ **On the piss:** out drinking.
- ❖ **Piss artist:** a person who fools around or is feckless.
- ❖ **Pisshead:** confirmed or heavy drinker.
- ❖ **Pisshole:** an unpleasant place.
- ❖ **Piss-take:** parody or send-up.
- ❖ **Piss-poor:** of extremely poor quality.
- ❖ **Pissed:** drunk

PEE

Pee has just enough daring to flaunt the first letter but too much decorum to use the full family name. Authors who tire of prim urine may hazard a *pee* when the context permits informality. It came into its own in the nineteenth century, when Victorians were as fond of covering up words as piano legs. However, Shakespeare's sly punning in the unwitting mouth of Malvolio in *Twelfth Night* ('By my life this is my lady's hand: these be her very Cs, her Vs, and her Ts, and thus makes

she her great Ps') suggests the euphemism was already thriving
a couple of centuries earlier.

PIDDLE

Before it was co-opted as a nursery euphemism, *piddle* enjoyed a
blameless life toying with food and pecking, with antecedents
relating to the regional German *piddlen* or *pitteln* (to pick at). Thus
Sir Richard Barckley's description of a dove in 1598 – 'There
commeth a dove flying towards him, and alighteth upon his
shoulder, and pidleth in his ear' – is not at all what you might think.

Sadly, by the end of the eighteenth century, birds are no longer
piddling but children are. Francis Grose records the new usage a
shade disdainfully in 1788: 'To Piddle, to make water: a childish
expression; as, Mammy, I want to piddle'. Its saving grace has been
to extend our lexicon of metaphorical water expressions, with
fountains and rain and taps cheerfully *piddling* through modern
English literature.

WEE

Adults embarrassed to find the childish *wee* in their urinary
vocabulary can take heart from the manly wordsmith Dylan
Thomas, who had it in his. 'Wee on the sun that he bloody well
shines not,' he wrote in 1934.

WEE-WEE

The photographer and dandyish socialite Cecil Beaton is credited
with first use of this one in print. 'Young men,' he noted in a camp
1930 diary entry, 'hurried into the garden to wee-wee.' These days
it's a favourite of potty-training mothers, who are sometimes
aghast to find it also slipping out at the office, possibly as they
excuse themselves from a board meeting.

WHIZZ

The writer D.H. Lawrence is thought to have first spotted the
onomatopoeic potential of *whizz*. In his 1929 poetry collection
Pansies we find the deathless lines: 'I wish I was a gentleman /As

full of wet as a watering-can / To whizz in the eye of a police-man.'
The book was banned on publication in England. Some sources
implicate the Old Norse *hvæsa*, to hiss.

WIDDLE

Widdle became fashionable in the 1950s, when it lined up with a
few of the sillier members of the tribe in John Pudney's humorous
survey of toilets, *The Smallest Room*, in 1954: 'The wee-wee, the
widdle, the pee-pee, and the piddle.' The alliterative symmetry
makes it clear why *widdle* joined the party, but Pudney didn't invent
the word. The naturalist Gerald Durrell's memories of childhood
in his 1956 autobiography, *My Family and Other Animals*, included
his brother Larry's suggestion that their puppies be named Puke
and Widdle.

LEAK

The American fondess for *leak* as a noun is of surprisingly recent
vintage. It was first recorded by the Oxford English Dictionary in
the colourless 'I stood there taking a leak' in Henry Miller's *Tropic
of Cancer* in 1934. But in Britain it has more robust antecedents as
a verb.

'Why, you will allow us ne're a jordan [chamber-pot], and then
we leake in your chimney,' banters one of the carriers in
Shakespeare's *Henry IV Part 2*. In 1731 Jonathan Swift had fun with
the word in *Strephon & Chloe*: 'Twelve cups of tea (with grief I speak)
/ Had now constrain'd the nymph to leak.' By 1796 it had itself
leaked into Francis Grose's ground-breaking *Classical Dictionary of
the Vulgar Tongue* ('To Leak: to make water') alongside such lost
treasures as 'Looking-glass: a chamber-pot, Jordan, or member-
mug'.

LAVATORY

Originally a vessel for washing and then a room with washing
facilities, from the Latin *lavatorium*, this is the word that's supposed
to give away our class. Not that most of us, in urgent need of
excusing ourselves from the Queen, would remember which way

to jump. Is *lavatory* the authentically posh choice, or does it merely expose you as a common *arriviste*?

According to Nancy Mitford, who unleashed an anxious national debate on the subject in the fifties, *lavatory* is indeed the one to keep in mind for Buckingham Palace, although she rules that *loo* is also acceptable. Her 1954 essay, 'The English Aristocracy', contained a glossary of U words (upper-class) and non-U (representing the aspiring middle-class). This consigned *toilet* to the non-U column, along with those unrelenting social markers *serviette*, *dentures*, *settee*, *perfume* and *pardon*.

In case you think these verbal class distinctions are an absurdity of the past, consider the fate of the mother of the future wife of the Queen's grandson, Prince William. In 2007 Kate Middleton's mother Carole, a former air hostess, was reportedly dissed by insiders at the Palace for asking to be excused to go to the toilet instead of the lavatory. 'She is incredibly middle-class,' moaned a horrified royal source.

Loo

This handy word has posed etymologists one of their most celebrated puzzles. Most suggestions founder on the inconvenient fact that the word is not recorded anywhere until James Joyce starts playing with it in the early twentieth century. Not that this has inhibited historical speculation.

One theory suggests a corruption of '*Gardez l'eau*', the cry from above which alerted passersby to the imminent emptying of chamber-pots into the street in medieval times. Another theory blames the seventeenth-century French preacher, Louis Bourdaloue, whose sermons lasted so long that wealthier Parisian ladies had recourse to chamber-pots under their voluminous dresses[*]. English etymology has also attempted a hopeful stab in the dark, with nautical types suggesting an early corruption of *leeward*, the side of a vessel that has the wind working in your favour when you're taken short. The most plausible suggestion, given its first

---

See: Bourdaloue[*]

recorded foray into English in 1922, is that the French *lieux d'aisances*, literally places of ease, could have been picked up by British servicemen in the First World War and carried across the Channel.

But it could equally be the case that, far from enjoying an exotic conception in some impressive historical setting, *loo* is simply the accidental offspring of a pun. Certainly that is the sort of fun Joyce was having with it in his novel *Ulysses*, where he takes the word for its first eccentric outing in print: 'O yes, mon loup. How much cost? Waterloo. Watercloset.'

TOILET

It's a word that has plunged socially since its heyday as the seductive arrangement of a lady's hairdressing ensemble and its even earlier life as the cloth (French *toile*) that covered the shoulders while one's hair was being beautified. But at least the change of usage perked up a few English Literature classes: pupils disappointed to find that Aleander Pope's 1717 poem, 'The Rape of the Lock', is only about the theft of some hair at least got a snigger out of: 'And now, unveil'd, the toilet stands display'd / Each silver vase in mystic order laid.'

NETTY

The mysterious provenance of this sprightly dialect word for a urinal has set Geordie imaginations on fire. Could it be a shortened version of the Italian word for toilets, *gabinetti*? Might it have arrived with the Romans during their occupation of South Shields? Is there a chance that it came from graffiti on Hadrian's Wall? There is no evidence whatsoever, but hopeful speculation abounds.

A painting by Robert Olley in 1972, depicting an old *netty* once frequented by miners at Westoe in South Shields, became so famous that the original urinal was ultimately salvaged and put on display in the Beamish Museum. The painting, called *Westoe Netty*, shows a row of men in black jackets and cloth caps lined up in stalls in front of a wall decorated by graffiti, while a small boy in the middle has a cheeky pee into his neighbour's boot.

Bob Olley, a former miner known optimistically as the Geordie Lowry, opened the new exhibit at Beamish in 2008.

PRIVY

First used in the thirteenth century to denote any kind of lavatory or latrine, *privy* later came to mean an unplumbed outside toilet. It arrived in English from the Anglo-Norman *privé* bearing the sense of intimate, secret or exclusive, a meaning it carried from the Latin *privatus* – although the notion of a private place to do your business was alien to the Romans who rejoiced in multi-occupational latrines and chamber-pots so public you could carry on playing ball while engaged with one*.

The word lent itself to one of the seventeenth-century's pithier epigrams: 'A true friend should be like a Privie, open in time of necessity.'[1]

SPEND A PENNY

One of our fondest euphemisms, this is a reminder of the days when you had to slip a large copper penny into a slot to gain entrance to a cubicle in a public lavatory. The first public toilets were featured at London's Great Exhibition in 1851. The sanitary engineer and plumber, George Jennings, who invented the flush toilet years before the more famous Thomas Crapper, installed his water closets in the Retiring Rooms of the Crystal Palace to great excitement from visitors. For their penny, thrilled patrons received a clean seat, a towel, a comb and a shoeshine. Like *powdering your nose* or *pumping ship* (a gentleman's colloquialism borrowed from sailors' slang), *spending a penny*'s days as a genteel excuse are surely numbered.

ADDLE

Most of us confess to it without feeling unduly compromised. Even the nimble-witted Charles Dickens had no qualms about describing himself on a bad day as *addle-headed*. But the innocent-sounding

---

See: 𝔖lavish 𝔄ttentions*

addle is a deceptively experienced metaphor. It has been steeped in urine for a very long time.

The word is from the Old English *adela* (a stinking pool of pee) and came to be used of a decomposing egg that produces no chicken, copying the Latin *ova urinae* (egg of urine). Under its modern veneer of vaguely humorous confusion, we are being invited to contemplate an empty brain reeking of pee like a bad egg.

From the condition of an addle-egg – empty, rotten and unfit for purpose – grew the sense of muddle and confusion associated with an addle-brain. 'Thy head is as full of quarrels as an egg is full of meat,' Mercutio taunts his sparring partner Benvolio in Shakespeare's *Romeo and Juliet*, 'and yet thy head hath been beaten as addle as an egg for quarrelling.'

No word illustrates more pithily than *addle* the capacity of urine to pop up where you least expect it.

Alchemist's Reward

Urine led alchemists a weary dance. Hour after hour, century after century, it was inspected and strained, tasted and smelled, boiled and evaporated, in the hope that it might be the elixir that would turn base metals into gold. After all, it was the right colour. But in the end urine yielded up something quite different: not gold, but phosphorus – the first new chemical element in around 150 years.

Hennig Brandt was a Hamburg merchant and part-time alchemist who had served as a soldier during the Thirty Years War. In 1669 he was busy, as usual, trying to extract gold from urine. This time his experiment involved leaving fifty buckets of it to stand until it putrefied so badly that it bred maggots. He then boiled the urine and kept the residue in his cellar until it turned black. After that he distilled it and collected it under water in a flask, which gave him a transparent waxy substance. Hey presto. He took the material out of the water and, to his gratified amazement, it was glowing pale-green in the dark.

Brandt naturally thought he had found the fabled Philosopher's Stone, although subsequent experiments quickly put him straight. But he did possess the secret of a substance that gave off enough illumination to allow him to read his old alchemy works under its light. Some sources suggest it might even have been Brandt who first called it 'phosphorus', the name of the morning star, from the Greek for 'light-bearing'. We now know it came from inorganic phosphate, a component of dissolved urine solids. White phosphorus is highly reactive and gives off a faint greenish glow on uniting with oxygen.

Brandt eventually began showing his magical prize around, even making some to sell when he was out of pocket. Although he tried to keep the recipe secret, the news that urine was involved leaked out. Before long two rival alchemists, Johann Kunckel and Daniel Kraft, were passing off the wonder as their own. When Kraft demonstrated its astonishing properties in London in 1677, Robert Boyle – the father of modern chemistry – determined to extract it himself from urine, and eventually used white phosphorus to develop the first matchstick[*].

The age of the alchemists was passing, but urine's time for revealing its golden chemical secrets was just beginning.

Alum

IT IS ASTONISHING to realise that until the 1870s, urine was sloshing up and down the coast of Britain by boat, feeding the insatiable demands of a major British industry. Such enormous quantities were needed in north Yorkshire for the production of alum, a mordant used to fix dye to fabric, that a booming east-coast transport network developed.

Ships would carry coal from Newcastle or Sunderland to Whitby, offload the coal, fill up with alum and continue down the coast to London. There they would leave the alum at the docks and load the ship with barrels of urine collected from street corners in the capital. These then chugged up the coast to supply the alum works at Whitby before going back to Newcastle. It was an inspired commercial circle.

Until the sixteenth century England imported the alum needed

See: Icy Noctiluca[*]

for dyeing textiles from Italy. The big alum works at Tolfa, near Rome, were owned by the Vatican. When Henry VIII fell out with Rome over plans to divorce his first wife, Pope Clement VII lost no time in cutting off England's alum supplies. That started an urgent search for indigenous alum at home.

But the alum that had formed as a natural mineral in the warmer climate of Italy was not so easy to find in a workable form in England. For the rest of the century alum-hunters searched high and low for domestic sources, with little success. Even the promising Alum Bay on the Isle of Wight, harbouring clusters of potential seams in its rainbow cliffs, did not yield a sustainable alum works. Nobody, it seemed, had the right recipe.

Then, at the turn of the century, the remarkable Sir Thomas Chaloner from Guisborough enters the story. He was a true Renaissance man – scholar, tutor to King James's son Henry, soldier, textile entrepreneur – and such a sharp-eyed naturalist that when he noticed the leaves on his estate were tinged an unusual shade of green, he seems to have suspected the presence of alum. Since nobody in England knew how to prepare it, Sir Thomas (or possibly a cousin of his by the same name) visited the Vatican alum works in Tolfa to try and find out how it was done. The legend goes that after failing to wheedle the information out of the Italians, he smuggled two workers out of the factory in a couple of large casks and took them back to Guisborough.

The Pope, by this time Clement VIII, was so outraged by the theft of this fiercely guarded industrial secret that he excommunicated the fugitives with an imprecation, first coined by Bishop Ernulphus of Rochester, so comprehensive that it ran to more than a page of manuscript. It included the devout hope that they might be cursed 'in the hair of their heads, in their brain, in the forehead and in the ears, in their eyebrows and in their cheeks, in their jawbones and in their nostrils'.

However, Sir Thomas Chaloner's brain at least seems to have remained in fine fettle. With the help of his Italian workmen, he set out to wrest the longed-for dye-fixer from the alum deposits near Guisborough. Nowadays we commonly understand alum as the crystalline double sulphate of aluminium and either potassium or ammonium. Chaloner and his people were not in a position to understand the chemistry but they worked out empirically how to produce it. In that sense alum was the earliest chemical industry in the British Isles.

By heaping quarried alum shale into giant mounds and setting these to burn slowly on brushwood for up to a year, they produced ash that could then be dissolved in water. This freed the various sulphates, including aluminium sulphate. Then they figured out that if you added urine (a source of ammonia) or potash from burnt seaweed (a source of potassium), or indeed both, you would get a reaction between the aluminium sulphate and those two alkalis that produced alum crystals.

But how on earth did they find that out? Did someone pee on the solution by accident to glad shouts of 'Eureka'? We have no idea. All we can know for sure is that the Chaloner family set up an alum works at Belman Bank near Guisborough, which depended on urine and became so profitable that the mines were later commandeered by the Crown. It's rumoured that one of the reasons Chaloner's son (another Thomas) signed the execution warrant of Charles I was because he was still so furious at the way the Crown had deprived his father of the fruits of his innovation.

In the hunger for more alum shale, the industry gradually ate into the coastline from Saltburn and Loftus south to Ravenscar; even today the remains of a burning floor at Sandsend alum works, north of Whitby, retain the look of a lunar landscape. In its thirst for urine, though, the industry had to look even further.

At first it was collected locally in Yorkshire, but before long urine was being shipped to Whitby in what were called 'lye boats' from Newcastle, Hull and eventually London. As with Methodists' urine in the Welsh wool-making areas[*], Whitby urine was reputed to be ideal because so many locals were teetotallers. If it came from London, then the urine of the beer-drinking poor was supposedly preferred to the capital's wealthier wine-quaffers,

See: 𝖍𝖆𝖓𝖉𝖞 𝖕𝖆𝖓𝖉𝖞[*]

although it's hard to see how anyone could tell by the time it had been collected in anonymous buckets on the streets and mixed up in barrels for transportation.

It's been suggested that transporting this bizarre freight from port to port was the origin of the expression 'taking the piss'.[4] Though this sounds a little too good to be true, the cargo was certainly crucial to the economy. In the last two months of 1612 alone, 16,000 gallons of farm urine from the surrounding countryside and 13,000 gallons of London urine were taken from Whitby to the alum works at Sandsend.

In the second half of the nineteenth century alum began being extracted from colliery waste and the vast alum shale quarries became redundant. Thus concluded a story that spanned two-and-a-half centuries and encompassed a king's divorce, a knight's industrial espionage, a pope's curse and, close to its heart from beginning to end, an awful lot of urine.

Anzart Melodies

THE EDINBURGH FESTIVAL is wearily accustomed to civic outrage over nudity, sex and four-letter words. In 1984 it held its breath for the uproar as a naked New Zealander prepared to spend a long evening urinating in public to create melodies on drums. The startling performance by John Cousins, a sculptor and composer from Christchurch, gave the Edinburgh Festival its first official 'piss-artist'.

'Membrane' was part of an ANZART exhibition, celebrating the work of Australian and New Zealand artists. Stretched out naked on a tilted bench with perspex tubes attached to his body, Cousins lay for seven hours in front of a wide-eyed public, inhaling air and imbibing water at one end and expelling urine at the other. The droplets of urine were directed via a foot-operated pump on to the rubber membranes of seven drums, which beat to the rhythm of his body. He said his inspiration came from the sound of dripping water in a New Zealand canyon. To ensure peak performance, Cousins fasted for four days before the show and drank eighteen to twenty mouthfuls at a time during it. The audience moved through in groups of fifteen, waiting agog for the water to work its way round his system and his kidneys to do their work. Then the drumming would resume.

Spectators seemed to find it strangely compelling. The tableau of transparent tubes and suspended domes, with a naked figure at the centre producing his uncanny music as light spilled through the window from Edinburgh Castle, was described by somewhat dazed festival-goers as 'spectacular'. The controversy evaporated and the strange artistry of the performance proved a success. 'It was halfway between a medical experiment and a piece of music, and done with the most incredible dignity,' the organiser Richard Demarco recalls. 'You were left with the sense that music comes from the business of being human, that with every breath we're in harmony with the most basic rhythms.' After the performance John Cousins was reported by friends to be 'very tired'. He declined to talk to reporters, who slunk off to look for a new sensation.

Around the House

BEFORE CHEMICAL DETERGENTS were available, housewives had a plentiful source of their own at home. Porcelains, saucepans, grimy ovens, kitchen floors, clothes with stubborn stains – nothing could beat the ammonia in stale urine for binding with fatty deposits and lifting off the dirt. It could give a streak-free shine to windows to satisfy even the most house-proud.

In wealthy pre-industrial households, the job of collecting the urine fell to below-stairs staff. According to British housekeeping guides, one of the younger male servants would have the job of fetching the teeming bedpans and storing the contents while they aged. Once it was nicely pongy, the urine would be dispensed either to the laundry or the mop-bucket.

The domestic employment of urine crosses classes and cultures. A woman born in 1857 in the Húnavatnssýsla district of Iceland used to regale youngsters with the story of how, when she was young, clothes and bedlinen were washed in old, heated urine and then rinsed with water. The urine not only cleaned them but bleached them a beautiful white, she said. Icelanders at that time, predominantly farmers, also used fresh urine to wash their hands.

More specialised uses included an inspired innovation by the Inuits, who created steam baths by urinating on hot stones in an enclosed tent. A Native Indian tribe, the Pericui, are said to have made a varnish of pee and coal dust to coat their children's faces as armour against the weather.

There are those today who swear by peeing on a car windscreen to de-ice it or, assuming a keen aim, into a frozen keyhole. Some cyclists are fans of urinating on their hands to warm them up in winter. The English golfer Tony Jacklin reports being assured by his father that the same hand trick would harden the skin and make him play better – although given urea's proven success as a moisturiser*, Jacklin senior was possibly joking.

Asparagus

WHEN IT COMES to urinary odour, asparagus is the king of vegetables. Mercifully, however, only half the population will ever know it. Scientists have still not pinpointed the compound that makes the urine of some asparagus eaters a bit whiffy: mercaptan, thioesters and aspargusic acid are all in the frame here. But they do know that who is affected is a matter of genetics. Around fifty per cent of us have a gene that produces the digestive enzyme responsible for breaking down the compound in asparagus that gives smelly pee. The rest of us can munch on with impunity. Even more intriguingly, only those who possess this particular gene can smell anything awry anyway.

The pong has been compared to rotten cabbage. Not all that enticing, you would think, especially as mercaptan is the same compound that gives skunks their offensive odour. But some sufferers beg to differ, including the prolix French novelist Marcel Proust, who described in *Swann's Way* how a dinner of asparagus had changed his chamber-pot into 'a jar of fragrance'.

See: **Skin** *

Bananas

So, ARE ANDREAS SLOMINSKI'S bananas filled with urine or not? Merely by audaciously claiming that they are, the German artist has boosted the value of a bunch of mottled fruit to a reputed £15,000.

Slominksi, who specializes in absurdist riddles and faintly slapstick art, first became famous for planting a sawn-off tree-stump in Berlin's iconic Unter den Linden lime-tree boulevard, prompting a police investigation. His works often explore the potential for deception, and none more maddeningly than the one he created in 1994 labelled *Ohne Titel (untitled)*, *Bananas, urine (injected)*. Exhibited in the Scottish National Gallery of Modern Art in July 2009, the bunch lay casually on a windowsill, looking much like six ordinary bananas. Which they may well have been. Except that Slominski says not.

His teasing artist's certificate left some exhibition visitors baffled and others furiously unimpressed by the German sense of humour. The work's exorbitant value lies solely in the shock of what that certificate says, since the curators of the Edinburgh gallery had to replace the ripening bananas every few days themselves. They smugly refused to reveal whether or not they did any urine-injecting of their own on their way back from the greengrocer.

Slominski himself can afford to laugh at the reaction his work provoked in Edinburgh. After all, an art collector by the name of Alexander Schröder paid real money for those bananas – although naturally he only bought them for the label.

Bashful Bladder

THE FEAR OF urinating in public has bred a diverse family of names for the condition, from the retiring Bashful Bladder to the official Paruresis. Others include Shy Kidney, Pee Shyness (or its near cousin Shy Pee), Urophobia, Shy Bladder Syndrome and, grandest of all, Psychogenic Urinary Retention.

Whatever the name, it is a more debilitating and widespread condition than you might imagine at first snigger. Sufferers visiting a crowded toilet are affected by a heart-thumping paralysis. Whether the anxiety is brought on by invasion of personal space, concern about exposure, fear of being rushed or worry about being overheard, some people simply cannot venture into the Ladies or Gents without panicking; others can't bring themselves to go near a public toilet at all.

A research paper presented to a British Psychological Society conference in 2005 claimed the condition affects as many as one in ten people. This sounds improbably high, although it's possible the researchers were counting the kind of off-on experience that the London journalist Hugo Rifkind described in a column for *The Times*. Having found himself at a urinal next to the British celebrity broadcaster Jonathan Ross, Rifkind confided: 'At first I couldn't go, but then I had a sort of morale boost because I noticed that he couldn't go either, so I suddenly could go, and then I walked away. He was still there. Getting nowhere. Awkwardly starting to hum.'

Rifkind's heartfelt conclusion – 'God, it must be awful being famous' – would have struck a chord with the movie actor John Wayne, who said the worst thing about stardom was when the guy standing next to you at a urinal turned and said: 'Say, aren't you John Wayne?' There are no statistics on celebrities who dry up in urinals but their experiences must be upping the bashful bladder count.

Serious sufferers clearly have a real problem, although the difficulty of judging a genuine claim was illustrated by the case of the Hungarian athlete Robert Fezekas. He was stripped of his gold medal in the men's discus at the 2004 Athens Olympics after failing to produce a urine sample and then leaving the testing facility early. He claimed to be suffering from paruresis and said he was unable to urinate under observation. Since anti-doping rules don't cater for the condition*, his defence cut no ice.

There are compensations, though. The UK Paruresis Trust says inability to urinate in public has occasionally been accepted as a valid reason for being excused from jury service. It also reports success in getting incapacity benefit restored to someone who was unable to urinate away from home.

Some nationalities are particularly prone to social trauma in this area. The Japanese cause themselves such agonies of embarrassment that the Tokyo-based toilet manufacturers, Toto, have introduced a model with an inbuilt sound system which plays watery noises to encourage those who are too self-conscious to start at their own behest.

Beer

ANYONE WHO HAS ever complained of being served beer that tastes like piss is closer to an ancient brewing truth than might be realised. From the time beer was introduced to Britain in the fifteenth century from Germany and Flanders, taverns were cheerfully adding urine to make a stronger ale. By the seventeenth century the process had even evolved its own verb, *leint*, to describe the process of mingling the ale with *lant*, the old word for stale urine**.

The literature of the time fairly reeks with references to the practice. The eponymous Tinker of Turvey claims in 1630 to have 'drunke double-lanted ale, and single-lanted'. Thirty years later the anonymous Renaissance drama, *The Marriage Broker*, includes a

---

See: Sport*
    Words to the Wise, Lant**

lament that: 'My hostess takings will be very small, / Although her lanted ale be nere so strong.' John Wright's burlesque *Mock-Thyestes* in 1674 has a character 'dead drunk with double lanted ale' and by 1691 the practice is so common that it wins a place in John Ray's *North Country Words*: 'To leint ale: To put urine into it to make it strong.'

But not everyone approved. The brewers' bible, *The London and Country Brewer*, complained in 1743 of the 'nasty, horrid and detestable piece of cunning and knavery … of putting chamberly, or human urine, into their pale or amber twopenny malt drink'. No doubt the practice continued but taverners kept quiet about it.

These days enough people still believe that beer and urine have a more intimate relationship than decency warrants for the mere rumour of a liaison to cause panic. In the 1980s a Heineken distributor in Nevada had the machiavellian idea of spreading the rumour that workers at a rival Corona brewery in Mexico were relieving themselves into Corona's popular light lager, before it reached customers in the States. The hoax proved wildly successful. As the rumour seeped across the country, shops began hauling Corona beer off their shelves and sales plunged.

Eventually, Corona traced the rumour to the Heineken wholesaler Luce and Sons, of Reno, and sued them for $3 million. An out-of-court settlement was reached in July 1987, when Luce agreed to state publicly that Corona beer was not contaminated with urine. However, it took years for sales to recover. Rarely in the history of bar-room slander can 'It tastes like warm piss' have proved so costly.

Beeting the Colour

THERE ARE NO statistics on the number of GP visits triggered by beetroot-eaters convinced they are dying but there must be a research grant in it for someone.

Beetroot contains pigments known as betacyanins, which can turn urine red. The exact hue will depend on the acidity of your stomach. The less acidic it is, the less likely the beetroot colour will be broken down in your gut, and the more likely that your pee will emerge flamboyantly crimson. Those who rush to the doctor to report that their urine has turned blood-red will face the embarrassment of being quizzed about the salad at last night's dinner. Rhubarb and blackberries can have the same effect.

Sadly, a suggestion that Roman togas were sent back from the laundry slightly pink in the salad season[*] is probably apocryphal.

Blasphemy?

NEW YORK-BORN Andres Serrano's photograph of a plastic crucifix from which the figure of Christ hangs, submerged in a glass of the artist's urine, caused uproar in the United States in 1989. The problem was not just that it was provocatively titled *Piss Christ* but that it had been publicly funded to the tune of $15,000.

Opponents of the federal funding body, the National Endowment for the Arts, thrilled at having this 'morally reprehensible trash' in their sights. The *Arizona Republic* argued that the NEA would have refused to fund Serrano if he had placed an image of Martin Luther King in a jar of urine, and the tele-evangelist Pat Robertson denounced it as 'blasphemy paid for by the government'. *Piss Christ's* celebrity was assured when Senator Alphonse D'Amato tore up a copy in the Senate.

Serrano himself didn't consider the work blasphemous. And although it has continued to stir religious controversy, some Christians regard it as a legitimate statement about what contemporary society has done to Christ, others as an exploration of the boundaries between the sacred and the profane.

Andrew Hudgins argues in his poem 'Piss Christ' that if we didn't know the artist had used cow's blood and urine, or that the cross was gimcrack plastic, we would see the work as a beautiful image: Christ – 'skidding into this world as we do / on a tide of blood and urine' – transformed into light at the Resurrection. What we see in Serrano's picture, he argues, is 'the whole irreducible point of the faith, / God thrown in human waste, submerged and shining'.

See: **Romans**[*]

𝔅lue 𝔐onday

SO IMPORTANT WAS urine to the craft of dyeing that medieval dyers rarely had their hands out of it. The stench of their clothes and the stain of blue woad dye on their fingernails[*] earned them the contemptuous epithet Blue Nails and contributed to a life of social exclusion that kept some out of textile guilds and forced others to flit from city to city in search of work.

In Germany the Blue Nails are said to be behind the popular expression *Blauer Montag*. A Blue Monday is the sort of day when you feel like staying away from work (much the way the Manchester band New Order seemed to feel in their dreary 1983 hit single of the same name).

Monday is said to have been when German dyers had their day off, having left a giant vat of woad and urine to ferment on the Sunday evening. The story goes that they knocked back such copious quantities of ale over the weekend that they were too hungover to do much anyway the next day. Thus did 'blue' come to be associated with over-indulgence and a strong desire to go back to bed on a Monday morning.

It's true this derivation is disputed. But in the absence of a definitive origin of Blue Monday, perhaps we can just give it to the oft-despised dyers, whose mastery of an ancient craft brought a blaze of colour to medieval life and vivid ostentation to the court of kings – even if they did smell of old pee.

𝔅ourdaloue

IT IS UNFORTUNATE that a man who held audiences spellbound by the fire of his rhetoric, the mellifluous loveliness of his voice and the accessibility of his theological expositions to the simple as well as the wise, should be remembered for giving his name to a chamber-pot.

In seventeenth-century Paris, Louis Bourdaloue's name was mentioned in the same breath as leading men of letters like

---

See: 𝔚oad[*]

Corneille and Racine. In an age when the great preachers of Europe were crowd-pulling celebrities, Bourdaloue was in the superstar league. Called frequently to Versailles to deliver his sermons before Louis XIV, the Jesuit preacher from Bourges soon became known as 'king of preachers and preacher of kings'.

So popular were his sermons that the ladies of the court used to arrive hours before he was due to start in order to secure a seat. It could be such a long wait that their maids would bring with them a neat, oval-shaped chamber-pot, often decorated with flowers, that had been specially designed for women to urinate in from a squatting or standing posture. Under the voluminous dresses of the day this could be achieved with discretion.

Bourdaloue's popularity is the kindest interpretation. Other sources suggest it was the inordinate length of his sermons, brilliant though they might have been, which put pressure on the bladders of the congregation. It's also been mooted that the preacher, who suffered from a defect of the urethra that can make male urination messy, may have had recourse to the vessel himself – although why he should have wanted it decorated with flowers is anyone's guess.

One way or another, the name of this scintillating orator attached itself forever afterwards not to a winning style of exposition but to an aristocratic French chamber–pot.

Buses

SHEEP URINE, IMPROBABLY enough, is helping buses to reduce their harmful fuel emissions. Britain's Stagecoach company was among the first to spot the green potential of the urea going to waste in farmyards up and down the country. While the pork-loving Danes have concentrated on pig urine[*], it's sheep that have caught the fancy of Stagecoach. The company believes their pee, collected and refined into urea by the fertiliser industry, can improve air quality.

Stagecoach fitted one of its buses in Winchester with a tank containing urea straight from the farmyard. The ammonia reacts

See: Danish Blues[*]

with harmful nitrous oxides in the exhaust fumes and converts them to nitrogen gas and water, which are released as steam. Stagecoach South proclaimed proudly: 'It will help make our cities better places to be for the public.'

Buttered flips

LONG BEFORE JOINING the more *outré* reaches of alternative medicine*, a draught of urine was cheerfully prescribed by otherwise orthodox physicians.

Buttered flips were a homely children's medicine favoured by Richard Hazeltine, a nineteenth-century American doctor from Maine.

They consisted of recently passed urine from one of the children, some hot water, honey and a little butter. In 1819 Dr Hazeltine described the elixir in a letter as 'steeming' and 'salutiferous' and recommended it for children suffering from catarrh. He also drew his correspondent's attention to the health benefits of the 'Salem flip', a mixture of urine and molasses. This was the medicinal tipple of an elderly, very respectable Quaker lady from Massachusetts, he wrote, who enjoyed an excellent reputation as a nurse.

Dr Hazeltine may not have been so daft. The makers of Buckley's Mixture, the phenomenally successful Canadian cough syrup invented in 1919, are happy to let it be known that it contains ammonium carbonate, which can be obtained from urine** but is now produced synthetically. In a notable example of reverse psychology, Buckley's markets itself as the worst-tasting remedy for coughs and sore throats in the business. Its slogan – 'It Tastes Awful. And it Works.' – has helped it to become a household name in Canada. Buttered flips probably tasted rather better.

It's also reported that before penicillin was available to treat diptheria, a gargle with urine was sometimes prescribed to prevent a fatal swelling of the larynx in children. Doctors in China dosed

---

See: Drinking It*
Yeast**

patients on the same principle for centuries. Like Dr Hazeltine, they found urine helpful for soothing sore throats and reducing catarrh. The Chinese also used it to strengthen the effect of medicinal herbs – a practice celebrated by the *Shang Han Lun*, a guide to cold and fevers written in AD 220 and the oldest complete medical textbook in the world.

In England the seventeenth-century scientist Robert Boyle, regarded as the first modern chemist and nobody's fool[*], noted urine's efficacy. 'I knew an ancient gentlewoman,' he wrote, 'who being almost hopeless to recover of divers chronical distempers … was at length advised, instead of more costly physick, to make her morning draughts of her own water; by the use of which she strangely recovered, and is, for aught I know, still well.'

For aught anyone knows, Dr Richard Hazeltine's young patients recovered too. Exactly how much the urine was responsible, and how much the hot water and honey, has never been put to the test.

See: Icy Noctiluca[*]

Cabbages and Roses

EATING UP YOUR greens was important to Marcius Porto Cato the Elder. For the Roman statesman and soldier (234–149 BC), cabbage produced simply wonderful urine. 'It surpasses all other vegetables,' he enthused in *De Agricultura*, his engaging dissertation on farming life. The urine it gives you is 'wholesome for everything'.

Bathe a baby in it and the child will never be weakly, says Cato. Splash your eyes in it and you will see better. Apply it heated to your head or neck and you'll relieve any pain there. And if you're a woman, rejoice in a treatment just for you: 'If a woman will warm the privates with this urine, they will never become diseased.'

Now that the antiseptic qualities of urea are well attested[*] and the modern nursing mother has learned to soothe inflamed breasts by popping a cabbage leaf down her bra, there is less to sneer at here than at first sight. But Cato's thoughtful advice about how exactly a woman should prepare to warm her private parts in the cabbagey urine is more challenging: 'The method is as follows. When you

See: **Skin**[*]

have heated it in a pan, place it under a chair of which the seat has been pierced. Let the woman sit on it, cover her, and throw garments around her.'

We'll think about it, Marcius. In any case, the women of ancient Rome may have been too busy drinking turpentine to bother with cabbage. It's said the distilled pine-resin made their urine smell like bunches of roses. While the scent might have been an improvement, it's difficult to see how even the most fragrant pee would compensate for endangering your skin, eyes, lungs, central nervous system and kidneys, not to mention the likelihood of setting yourself on fire.

Cats

THE TENACIOUS STINK of their urine on the carpet is responsible for the untimely demise of more cats than a host of common maladies, including feline leukaemia and feline immune deficiency. Vets say it is the main reason they are put down or left at a shelter. Could it be the cat's background as a desert animal that makes its urine stains so downright smelly and difficult to neutralize? Having evolved to conserve water in the hot wastes of Egypt, where they were once fervently worshipped, cats produce urine said to be ten times more concentrated than the human or canine variety.

Chaperone

WHOEVER SNATCHED THIS pretty French word for a protective companion of respectable young ladies and stuck it on an escort whose job is to observe complete strangers dropping their pants must have had a lively sense of irony.

But as more and more volunteers are recruited to support the work of official drug testers, the name has stuck. Chaperones escort athletes to doping control stations and in some countries witness the collection of a sample. Their training is faintly surreal. For the Vancouver Winter Olympics in 2010[*] volunteers learned how to look an athlete straight in the eye (to start with, anyway) and rap out the mantra: 'Raise your shirt and drop your shorts to your

See: Sport[*]

knees. Turn round 360 degrees and then urinate in the test cup. You must remain in front of me the whole time.'

As the chaperones (or doping control officers, depending on how different national organisations manage their sample collection) nervously approach their first urinary assignment, they will probably know the blunt World Anti-Doping Agency guidelines off by heart:

❖ The Witness (DCO or Chaperone) shall escort the Athlete to the toilet facility.
❖ The Athlete shall be encouraged to wash his/her hands before providing a sample.
❖ Once in the toilet facility the Athlete must remove all clothing between the waist and mid-thigh, in order that the Witness has an unobstructed view of sample provision. Sleeves should be rolled up so that the Athlete's arms and hands are also clearly visible.
❖ The Witness shall directly observe the Athlete provide the urine sample, adjusting his/her position so as to have a clear view of the sample leaving the Athlete's body.
❖ The Athlete should be encouraged to fill the collection vessel.[5]

It's not a job everyone would relish. UK Anti-Doping, the national agency which conducts around 7,500 tests a year across 45 sports, pays an average £70 for a six-hour shift. Worth every penny, you might think, since as well as a steely courtesy and a strong stomach, volunteers need large reserves of patience and a thick skin. More than half the tests are done immediately after an event. So if you are meeting a dehydrated cyclist after a gruelling mountain race, you may have to dog his or her footsteps for five or six hours before anything can be produced in the doping control toilet. You are unlikely to feel loved.

But chaperones declare that the tedium of waiting, and the excruciating awkwardness of watching people pee, is worth it to help stop the cheats[*]. Scott Lowell, a doping control officer for the

_____
*See: **Sport**[*]

United States Anti-Doping Agency, believes in the mission with almost religious zeal. As he hovers near the Charles River in Boston at 6 a.m. to pounce on a rower hoping to compete in the London Olympics in 2012, he insists: 'I wouldn't be doing this if I didn't feel passionate about it.'

His randomly selected target, 23-year-old Yale graduate Alex Rothmeier, eases himself out of his boat at 7.15 a.m., notices the waiting USADA-embossed bag of collection cups, glass vials, sealed Styrofoam boxes and refractometer, and sighs. Barely hydrated after several hours of sleep and two hours rowing, he has no idea how long it will take him to produce the 90ml of urine that Lowell is after.

Lowell says the longest he has had to follow an athlete around was close to five hours. 'I've gone out to breakfast with guys, gone to their little kid's softball games, watched a couple of Red Sox games with athletes. Everything.'

Having undergone a rigorous selection and training process, he has now fitted more than a thousand urine tests (at $100 to $150 a go) around his day job as an account manager for a healthcare company. As he waits for Alex Rothmeier to hydrate himself, he explains why it matters.

'I've seen guys in January when this river is frozen and they are doing two-a-day, four-hour sessions busting their tails upstairs in the workout room. When you see that, you want to make sure what they are doing is worth it and they are not going to get beat by some doper.'

Maybe the word *chaperone* has found itself a respectable new life after all.

Churchill

PISSING ON A vanquished enemy is an ancient rite of conquest that seems never to have lost its atavistic appeal. Winston Churchill so enjoyed pissing on Germany in the final months of the Second World War that he did it twice.

First he chose the West Wall, the German defensive barrier known to the Allies as the Siegfried Line, which had been breached by the Allies as they advanced into Germany. With Hitler's war machine tottering, the British Prime Minister flew into Eindhoven in Holland in March 1945 and was driven by Rolls Royce to the American Ninth Army HQ to meet the US commander, Lieutenant General William Hood Simpson. Before the party moved on, Simpson asked Churchill if he would like to use the lavatory.

Churchill's military adviser, Field Marshall Sir Alan Brooke, recalled later: 'Without a moment's hesitation [Churchill] asked "How far is the Siegfried Line?" On being told about half an hour's run he replied that he would not visit the lavatory, but that we should halt on reaching the Siegfried Line.'[6]

The column of 20 to 30 cars duly pulled up at the fortifications near Aachen, beside rows of anti-tank defences known as 'dragon's teeth' and some pillbox bunkers recently blown up by the Americans. Brooke reports that the Allied top brass 'processed solemnly out and lined up along the line'. Photographers surged forwards but Churchill stopped them in their tracks. 'This is one of the operations connected with this great war which must not be reproduced graphically,' he announced loftily.

Churchill performed the ritual with relish. 'I shall never forget the childish grin of intense satisfaction that spread all over his face as he looked down at the critical moment,' wrote Brooke.

The photograph that Churchill did allow – of Allied leaders on the cusp of victory striding gravely among the serried rows of dragon's teeth – became one of the most famous of the war. The antics that accompanied it never reached the public's attention.

Three weeks later, Churchill directed a second jubilant stream into the River Rhine, a couple of days after British troops had forced their way across. He may have been trying to emulate the US General George S. Patton, who had relieved himself into the Rhine with similar gusto a few days earlier[*]. Churchill was never a man to let the Americans get one over him.

See: 𝓟atton[*]

Cinema Alert

YOU'RE IN THE middle of a film and beginning to suspect that the giant cola was a mistake. How do you manage your escape without missing a crucial plot twist and then annoying your neighbours by demanding a whispered *resumé* on your return?

A website called RunPee.com offers a whacky solution for selected films by suggesting the best point to make your dash. For instance, in the unlikely event that you were anxious not to miss the next grotesque despatching of a cardinal in the 138 minute-long movie of Dan Brown's thriller *Angels and Demons*, RunPee advises that you should pop out one hour and ten minutes in. That's the moment when the power goes out in the Vatican archives, trapping Tom Hanks and his guard without oxygen.

'This is the perfect time to Runpee,' we are assured, 'because they don't even talk much. You won't be missing a thing.' Believe me, you won't.

You then have three minutes grace, with the missing moments helpfully summarised. The service is also available as an iPhone application, allowing you to read it on the way back to your seat. It would, of course, be considerably less trouble just to go before the film starts.

Cliff Richard

CLIFF RICHARD WAS on stage at London's Hackney Empire, smouldering moodily. 'Curl your lip!' hissed producer Jack Good, as the cameras rolled. Cliff curled an obedient lip. 'Grab your arm as if you've been prodded by a syringe!' ordered Good a few bars later. Cliff gripped his left arm with his right and glowered. The teenage girls in the audience went wild. There was not a dry seat in the house.

Excitable mass peeing, later to reach its apogee with the Beatles, was as new a phenomenon in Britain as Good's *Oh Boy!* shows themselves, which went out live on ITV every Saturday in the late 1950s. The raw energy of rock n' roll was electrifying.

Marty Wilde, Billy Fury and Tommy Steele were among the

performers who launched their careers there, but it was the slinky-hipped young Cliff Richard who proved most effective at opening the audience floodgates. On 2 May 1959 he provoked hysteria with a couple of new songs, 'Choppin' n' Changin'' and 'Dynamite'. His finale with Marty Wilde and that week's special guest, Alma Cogan, had the teenagers swooning.

'The screaming from the girls was unbelievable,' recalled Stan Edwards, a former Butlins redcoat, who was watching open-mouthed from the gallery. Stan loved the atmosphere, which was a long way from anything he had experienced in the Butlins camp at Clacton, but, as caretaker, he had to clean the seats afterwards and wasn't so keen on what he used to find once the audience had clattered out.

Much more agreeable were the legendary *Take Your Pick* and *Emergency Ward 10*, both filmed at the Hackney Empire. The seats during these broadcasts are thought to have remained in better order.

Clochemerle

URINE TAKES PRIDE of place in more works of literature than we might think entirely wise[*]. Among them, Philip Roth created a character in *My Life as a Man* who tricks her husband into marriage by buying a urine sample from a pregnant stranger and switching it before her own pregnancy test (exactly as Roth claims his first wife did to him). Then there's the plot of John Irving's *The Water Method Man*, which hinges on the hero's abnormally narrow urinary tract. And we shouldn't forget Philip Larkin's poems, full of piss one way or another. But the French classic *Clochemerle* carries off the theme with particular aplomb.

Gabriel Chevalier's novel is a rollicking epic about the controversy that explodes in the French wine-growing village of Clochemerle when the ambitious mayor decides to erect a public urinal. In a community that has happily done without one for a thousand years and where diversions are few, he knows he will have a battle on his hands.

See: Ulysses, Gulliver's Travels, Rabelais[*]

As Mayor Piéchut observes, men who 'from generation to generation had relieved themselves against the foot of walls or in hollows in the ground' would be deprived of indulging 'such little whims and fancies as that of a jet well aimed that drives away a green fly, bends a blade of grass, downs an ant, or tracks down a spider in his web.'

Mindful of the importance to the men of Clochemerle of enjoying this pleasure 'openly and merrily', the mayor perversely decides to place the urinal directly in front of the village church and under the nose of the local curtain-twitching spinster. Soon the whole village is divided into Urinophobes and Urinophiles, old feuds and rivalries are reignited, a near-riot ensues in the church and the urinal becomes the target of a dynamite attack.

Chevalier's lampoon was a bestseller in France in 1934. He later adapted it for Pierre Chenal's 1947 movie, *Clochemerle*, which predictably ran into censorship trouble with the Americans, who rarely line up to appreciate urinal humour[*]. The book's heavy irony feels dated these days. Still, it is no mean feat to put urine at the heart of a novel and keep your readers with you.

Cocaine

IT IS DIFFICULT to monitor drug abuse accurately. Options include conducting a population survey (interminable), consulting crime statistics (inconclusive) or questioning the addicts (unreliable). Or you might try something entirely different. You can now sample wastewater in sewage or rivers and get the whole story from urine, the source that rarely lies.

Researchers proved this in 2008, when they measured residues from cocaine, opiates, cannabis and amphetamines at waste treatment plants in Milan, London and the Swiss city of Lugano. They used the amounts collectively excreted in urine to estimate consumption of the active parent drugs.

Cocaine residue was particularly easy to detect. Half of every dose is excreted as the byproduct benzoylecgonine and a small

_____
See: **Kisses!**[*]

percentage emerges as the unchanged drug itself. The urine footprint of cocaine users revealed that consumption was higher in Milan than either London or Lugano. It even showed cocaine use rising significantly in the Italian city every weekend, while heroin and cannabis remained steady across the week.

Amphetamine and cannabis consumption, on the other hand, was found to be higher in London than Milan, as was heroin. After morphine prescribed for pain relief was removed from the calculation, the amount recovered from urine showed 70mg of heroin a day was being consumed for every 1,000 people in Milan and 100 mg in Lugano. London streaked ahead with 210mg of heroin consumed every day per 1,000 people.

In an earlier study the same Italian researchers had used samples of water from the River Po to establish that far higher levels of cocaine were being deposited from urine than official statistics had suggested. Italy's largest river was found to be carrying the equivalent of about 4kg of cocaine every day, implying consumption of 40,000 doses of cocaine per day in the Po valley. Far more than could be accounted for by the 15,000 users who admitted taking the drug at least once a month. It was all passing straight from the toilet, through treatment plants not geared to filtering the drug out, and into the river.

As to where it goes next, there is no undisputed evidence that drug residues in urine are finding their way back from the rivers of the world into drinking water supplies*. If contaminant levels keep rising, though, you do wonder how long it might be before some blameless citizens find themselves on tiny doses of illicit drugs without even knowing it.

See: Gender Bender*

Confederate Belles

IN THE AMERICAN Civil War southern women threw themselves gamely behind the Confederate cause. 'In no instance,' declared the *Selma Morning Reporter* in August 1863, 'have they ever faltered or hesitated for one moment to do everything to secure the salvation of the South.' Later that year the women of Selma, Alabama, went for broke. They opened their newspapers on 1 October to find an advertisement from one Jonathan Haralson, a dashing Selma lawyer who had opened a nitre works to supply saltpetre for making gunpowder, of which the Southern States were acutely short. Dung-impregnated earth was taken from caves, stables and outhouses, but it required more urine to make saltpetre[*]. His advert got straight to the point:

> The ladies of Selma are respectfully requested to preserve all their chamber lye collected about their premises for the purpose of making Nitre. Wagons with barrels will be sent around for it by the subscriber.

> (signed) Jon Haralson
> Agent Nitre and Mining Bureau

Mr Haralson duly sent his carts around the city. Cosseted Southern belles, who were already learning how to knit socks for soldiers and dye wool in walnut leaves, responded to this new challenge with enthusiasm. But Jonathan Haralson himself, a Baptist churchgoer who later became a respected judge, had to put up with some ribbing. The sight of the pee-wagons inspired a rollicking poem entitled 'Rebel Gunpowder' from a legal colleague, Thomas Wetmore.

> John Haralson! John Haralson!
> You are a wretched creature.
> You've added to this bloody war

See: **Gunpowder**[*]

a new and awful feature.
You'd have us think while every man
is bound to be a fighter,
That ladies, bless the dears,
should save their P for nitre.

John Haralson! John Haralson!
Where did you get the notion
To send your barrel 'round the town
to gather up the lotion?
We thought the girls had work enough
making shirts and kissing,
But you have put the pretty dears
to patriotic p_____g.

John Haralson! John Haralson!
Do pray invent a neater
And somewhat more modest mode
of making your saltpetre;
For 'tis an awful idea, John,
gunpowdery and cranky,
That when a lady lifts her skirts
she's killing off a Yankee.

Jonathan Haralson responded to these efforts with some doggerel
of his own. With a name like Wetmore, his friend had it coming.

The women, bless their dear souls,
And everyone for war,
To 'soldier boys' they'll give their shoes,
Their stockings by the score.
They'll give their jewels all away,
Their petticoats to boot,
They'll have saltpetre, or they'll shout
In earnest phrase – 'Wet more!'

The women, were it not for them
Our country would be lost.
They charm the world, they nerve our hearts
To fight at every cost.
What care they how our powder's made?
They'll have it, or they'll bore
Through mines or beds in stables laid,
And, straining, cry 'Wet more!'

Women, yes they stoop to conquer
And keep their virtue pure.
It is no harm to kill a beast
With chamber lye I'm sure.
But powder we are bound to have,
And this they've sworn before;
And if the needful thing is scarce,
They'll 'press' it and 'Wet more!'

The banter flew backwards and forwards but, crucially, Jonathan Haralson's enterprise succeeded. With the help of the belles of Selma, his nitre works helped supply the Confederates with ammunition during the last two years of the war. His enterprise lasted until Union troops captured the city on 2 April 1865 and destroyed the manufacturing engine of the South's resistance: the arsenal, ordnance centre, foundries, ironworks and the gunpowder and nitre works. Just one week later General Lee surrendered and the American Civil War was over.

Croydon

TYPHOID MARY, THE cook who notoriously infected fifty-three people (three of whom died) in early twentieth-century New York, was tragically outclassed in 1937 by a Croydon workman. By relieving himself inside a well that supplied the London borough's drinking water, the labourer unknowingly instigated a catastrophic typhoid epidemic that infected 341 people in Croydon and killed a horrifying forty-three of them.

The man had contracted the disease during service in the First World War and, like 'Typhoid' Mary Mallon, was a carrier of the deadly typhoid bacillus. He was among a workforce of eighteen working on the Addington well, which fed a million gallons of water a day into the corporation's reservoirs, serving up to 40,000 of Croydon's 250,000 population.

Each day the workmen were lowered down the well by rope in a makeshift barrel, left there to cut a tunnel and drawn up again four hours later. In case they were taken short, a bucket was sent down for the men to urinate in. As soon as this was half-full, it was supposed to be returned to the surface for emptying in the same makeshift barrel, padded around with a load of excavated chalk.

The inquiry report was scathing about this arrangement. 'The most elementary care would seem to dictate at least the use of a vessel which could be closed before being thrust out into the well shaft and hauled to the surface,' Harold Murphy, KC, noted sternly.[7]

Exactly how the carrier, known to the inquiry as Case A, infected the water supply was never conclusively established. Tests found the typhoid bacillus in his faeces but the report noted that it was much more difficult to detect in urine and that more than half of faecal carriers were likely to be urinary carriers as well. The men all swore there had been no infringement of the sanitation rules. That put the slop bucket in the frame.

The real tragedy proved to be not that a hapless labourer was excreting typhoid in his urine, but that while he was working down that well in September and October 1937, the chlorination system that would have killed the bacteria was turned off. The untreated water being pumped into houses and hospitals led to the largest water-borne outbreak of typhoid fever in Britain in the twentieth century.

The blame for the catastrophe was laid largely on the careless procedures of the Croydon authorities. Unlike Typhoid Mary, who still bears the ignominy of refusing to acknowledge her agency in infecting 53 people in New York, the unwitting Case A was left with his anonymity intact.

Dandelion

HOW SAD. A meadow flower with the most majestic of names has been dragged into the gutter by its potency as a diuretic. The dandelion gets its imposing French name, *dent de lion*, from its leaves, as jagged as a lion's teeth. But eating these leaves has such a powerful effect on the bladder that the great dandelion name has been usurped by upstart colloquialisms like *pissabed* and *pee-the-bed*. This is an international phenomenon: in France dandelions are called *pissenlit* and in Italy *piscialletto*; Americans favour *pissy-bed*.

Dandelions increase the flow of urine by stimulating the excretion of salts and water from the kidneys. It used to be claimed that children would wet the bed after merely touching one, although that seems unlikely. Full of nutrients and high in minerals like potassium, the plant's medicinal qualities have been celebrated for centuries. Other plants with diuretic qualities, like the buttercup and even the humble daisy, have also been called *pissabeds* from time to time. But the dandelion is the bed-wetting king.

Danish Blues

DENMARK HAS 20 million pigs. They make wonderful bacon but their urine is an environmental hazard. Ammonia emissions and noxious smells are such a problem that the Copenhagen government has imposed rigorous air quality controls, with human 'sniffers' employed to check odour levels near dwellings. Since 2007 farmers have been awarded 'odour units', with seven points worth of pig smell allowed near a small community but only one point for a stench wafting into a town or city. This tight control has restricted expansion of the country's pork industry.

However, salvation could be at hand for Denmark's pig producers. In one of the more elegant green solutions, a Danish company has developed a system that can turn pig urine into plastics. The urine is first collected under grates in the pig-pens. Then it is separated from the manure and quickly filtered to remove urea, a component in plastics. The company, Agroplast, then uses this natural urea, a compound of carbon, nitrogen, oxygen and hydrogen, to make plastic dinnerware and household goods.

The infant technology is being hailed as a triple green whammy, which could see the world's pig population leading the charge against environmental pollution. First, you're not digging up buried fossil fuels to produce urea from natural gas. Second, with countries like the United States now importing half the urea it uses, you can reduce shipping and fuel. Third, pig urine is efficiently disposed of before it goes stale.

This last is the key benefit for poor, air quality-challenged Denmark. With the urea strained out before the urine has time to turn into ammonia, bringing home the country's bacon may one day be accomplished without ponging out every house in the neighbourhood.

Drinking It

J.D. SALINGER, RECLUSIVE American author of *The Catcher in the Rye*, got to ninety-one on it. Morarji Desai, former Prime Minister of India, made it to ninety-nine on a pint a day. Sarah Miles, English star of *Ryan's Daughter*, is still going strong after more than thirty years of knocking it back morning and evening. 'It tastes like good beer,' she confides. 'You just swig it down. It tastes fine.'

So why do they do it? It's one thing to reach for a glug of urine as a last resort* but quite another to turn it into a beverage of choice when every instinct screams revulsion. Even applying it to wounds and spots** doesn't turn the stomach quite as viscerally as the idea of drinking the stuff.

Yet people in China, India, south-east Asia, Japan (where urine is still prescribed for asthma, diabetes and hypertension) and among the camel-owning tribes of the Sahara have been doing it for thousands of years, while in Europe and America accounts of the practice have also peppered the centuries***. Those who embrace it in the West today believe it has demonstrable benefits as an all-purpose medical treatment that can sort out just about anything, from the common cold to cancer.

That, of course, is the problem with urine therapy. How can one substance, no matter how richly loaded with minute traces of bio-chemicals, possibly stimulate the body to cure itself of more or less anything? The quasi-religious enthusiasm of some devotees doesn't help either.

On the other hand, there have been more serious investigations into the therapeutic effects of urine-drinking, or 'uropoty' (yes, really), than we might think. In the early twentieth century, before synthetic versions of many of the constituents of urine were available in drug form, a smattering of mainstream doctors were regularly encouraging patients to drink their own to cure illness.

See: Survival*
     Skin**
     Buttered Flips***

Charles Duncan MD, an energetic New York surgeon and genito-urinary specialist, claimed in 1918 that there were 'more than two thousand physicians scattered throughout the world' who employed what he called 'autotherapy' every day in both private and hospital practice.[8] He said one physician in Pennsylvania had used it in over six hundred cases, with such good results that he had 'practically discarded the use of vaccines'. Vets, he said, were employing it as well. Dr Duncan was roundly derided in some quarters, but he listed a number of clinical successes and staked his reputation on the claim that: 'Many pathogenic conditions ... are quickly cured by the therapeutic employment of urine alone.'

In Dresden a German paediatrician, Dr Martin Krebs, was intrigued enough by reports of the efficacy of urine to try injections on some of his own young patients. In a lecture in Leipzig in 1934 he reported: 'Through intramuscular injections of the patient's own urine, allergies and certain spastic conditions in children are remarkably improved. Extraordinary improvement can be seen with asthma and hay-fever ... I treated an eight-year-old boy with hay-fever by injecting 5cc of his own urine, and was surprised at the result. The boy immediately began breathing better, and in a few minutes the extreme redness of the eyes disappeared.'

Clinical observations of this kind are what leading advocates of urine therapy today would like us to focus on. American nutritionist Martha Christy has sought to publicise twentieth-century research into the therapeutic effects of components of urine – including the medicinal effects of urea[*] and the impact of urine extract injections on different types of cancerous tumours.

In a more thoughtful book than its excitable title suggests[9], she quotes a ream of scientific papers to argue that throughout the last century 'researchers sat in their laboratories and watched as simple urea or whole urine completely destroyed rabies and polio viruses, tuberculosis, typhoid, gonorrhoea, dysentery bacteria and cancer cells.' She also claims it relieved asthma, eczema, whooping cough, migraines, diabetes, glaucoma, rheumatoid arthritis and a

---

See: Skin[*]

host of other illnesses. Evidence, she says, that the public was never given.

The theory is that your urine provides a kind of snapshot of whatever is going on in your body at a particular time. All fine so far[*]. However, the theory goes on to suggest that, once reintroduced into your body, different urinal components act as a personally designed medicine, becoming in effect natural vaccines, hormone balancers, allergy relievers, anti-bacterial, antiviral and indeed anti-cancer agents, and so on.

While medical researchers have had positive results with some constituents of urine, it's difficult to find scientists who will go this far.

'The idea that there's some immune property in the urine is a little hard to understand, given that our gut is designed to break down all immunological substances,' says Dr James Dillard, a professor at Columbia University's medical school and author of *Alternative Medicine for Dummies*. Even some urine therapists believe it is only really effective when injected rather than quaffed.

Doctors do broadly concede that drinking urine will do you little harm, as long as it's dilute enough to avoid a high salt concentration and free of excreted drug medications which could have an adverse effect the second time round. But they do ask why the body was profligate enough to get rid of all these useful chemicals in the first place if it wants them back so badly. Believers argue back that the kidneys are merely expelling what is not immediately needed to preserve the balance of the blood at any one time.

As with many alternative treatments, urine therapy ultimately leaves you weighing up passionate personal testimony against profound professional scepticism. Martha Christy says urine helped to cure her of a string of chronic diseases that had proved impervious to drugs since childhood. The English naturopath John Armstrong claimed in his influential 1944 treatise *The Water of Life* that he had cured himself of diabetes and lung disease – and his

---

See: UK Biobank[*]

patients of just about everything else – by fasting for long periods on water and urine alone. (He also reported: 'the taste of healthy urine is not nearly as objectionable as, say, Epsom salts.') But in the absence of rigorous trials, claims like these are impossible to verify.

We are left wondering if Salinger and Desai and Miles, Armstrong and Christy, the long, colourful trail of eastern practitioners, Duncan and Krebs and doctors like them along with their patients, have all been deluding themselves. It's possible. After all, the well-attested power of panacea (which itself means 'all-healing') remains a medical mystery. Or could these people have tapped into a different kind of potential for healing that more recent medical science has yet to get its head around? That, too, is always possible.

Duchamp Fountain

WHAT DOES IT say about civilisation when a urinal is voted the most influential modern artwork of all time? We would have to ask the 500 art experts whose 2004 poll put Marcel Duchamp's *Fountain* ahead of works by Picasso and Matisse. But his innovation in creating artistic significance from an everyday object certainly marked the beginning of conceptual art.

Duchamp's stroke of genius was to buy a standard Bedfordshire urinal from the J.L. Mott Iron Works in New York, sign it R. Mutt (with deliberate shades of the cartoon strip Mutt and Jeff) and submit it to the Society of Independent Artists' 1917 exhibition. While it was kept out of sight during the show itself, rejected for being neither original nor art, it became celebrated for what Duchamp described as the shifting of artistic focus from physical craft to intellectual interpretation.

The original *Fountain* was lost, probably thrown out as rubbish, but years later Duchamp commissioned several reproductions. Eight signed replicas, made in 1964 from glazed earthenware to resemble the original porcelain, can be found in museums around the world. One of them fetched an eye-watering $1.7 million at Sotheby's in November 1999.

Naturally the temptation of using it for its original purpose has proved irresistible. The most persistent vandal was Pierre Pinoncelli, a French performance artist, who urinated into it during a show in Nîmes in 1993 and then attacked it with a hammer in the Dada show in Paris in 2006. Pinoncelli explained after his first arrest that he wanted to rescue the work from its inflated status and restore it to its original function. A gesture Marcel Duchamp might just have applauded.

Dye

IN THE STRANGE and wonderful craft of staining fabric with colour, urine was the dyer's elixir. For thousands of years the artists of dye stole colour from lichens and redcurrants, bracken and onion skins, heather, peat, gorse, seaweed and bog myrtle, insects and shellfish, animal and mineral – indeed from anything in the natural world which would yield a pigment.

Some dyestuffs clung naturally to cloth but others did better with a mordant, or fixing agent, for which urine was often used. Other dyestuffs[*] needed the chemicals in urine to produce the pigment itself.

Poring over a steaming vat of stale pee and other nasty chemicals was unpleasant labour, for which dyers were often unfairly reviled[**]. 'The hands of the dyer reek like rotting fish,' noted a waspish Greek writer. But they created great beauty as well.

The Stockholm Papyrus, a Greek manuscript discovered in a Theban grave in Egypt, contains recipes in use there between the first and third centuries. These include instructions on how to dissolve the alkanet plant in camel's urine to make the deep red colour fast and durable, and a mouth-watering recipe for boiling up the comarum herb in pig manure along with the urine 'of an uncorrupted youth'.

Even after industrially produced mordants like alum became

See: Indigo, Lichen, Woad[*]
   Blue Monday[**]

available[*], urine was still prized by dyers as the best agent for cleaning the wool. In 1834 Gloucestershire-born master dyer William Partridge, who had emigrated to America and set up as a dyestuff dealer in New York, published a lovingly fussy book[10] in which he praised urine as 'the material mostly used for scouring of wool'. As he explained: 'The volatile alkali, that part of the urine which combines with the grease and yolk, does not injure wool, unless it be in considerable excess, or too much heat be applied.'

Defining the kind of human urine that dyers prize most for cleansing, Partridge advises: 'Urine that is fresh voided will not scour well. That from persons living on plain diet is stronger and better than from luxurious livers. The cider and gin drinkers are considered to produce the worst, and the beer drinker the best.'

For cleaning fine wool, he recommends one bucket of urine to two buckets of water. 'Some wool requires more and some less of urine; if too much is used, the wool will be stringy and difficult to work; if too small a quantity, the yolk and grease will not be cleansed out of it … The urine should be old, and the water the softest that can be procured.'

Across the Atlantic the producers of Harris Tweed were putting the same principles into practice in their Hebridean cottage industry, where urine was still being used to scour cloth, release pigment and fix dye until the eve of the twenty-first century[**].

See: Alum[*]
      Harris Tweed[**]

Eau de Toilet

IT'S A BRACING JOB at times, being a trading standards officer. You never know what you'll find in the Chanel No. 5 bottles that some hopeful Del Boy is flogging down the market. More times then they care to count, it will turn out to be urine.

A splash of pee is a gift to rogue traders. It's the right colour, produces a mildly astringent sensation on the skin and is easier to come by than the pond-water that has also leaked into numerous perfumes. The delicate fragrance of pee seems to blend in just perfectly, too.

Trading standards officers know what to expect these days when they spot an amber bottle selling for half what it should. One bargain-priced Chanel No. 5 seized from a market stall at Finmere in Oxfordshire was immediately confirmed to contain urine. And the same scam has been reported all over the country. Test after test on fake scents reveals its growing popularity as a stabiliser.

'With perfume you really don't know what you're getting,' said Handley Brustad, a senior trading standards officer in Cardiff. The moral, obviously, is to avoid big-name perfumes at wee prices.

€co⸴Revolution

ALL ROUND THE world the seeds of revolution are sprouting, and here's why. Plants need nitrogen to help them grow. Urine is rich in nitrogen. Human beings are rich in urine. Leaders of the revolution have grasped the simple concept that recycling the nutrients in urine can save the water we currently waste to flush them away, reduce the energy we use to treat them and cut back on the chemical fertilisers we invite into the food-chain instead.

The Scandinavian nations have led the way. The Swedes feel so strongly about needless flushing that they inaugurated a Pee Outside Day in 1999. Two 'eco-villages' were founded as far back as 1994 – Understenshödjen in Stockholm and Björsbyn in the far north – in which houses and apartments were fitted with urine-separation toilets.

Sweden has at least 135,000 of these eco-toilets now, which work by channelling urine and faeces into different compartments and storing the urine. Local farmers collect as much as they need for fertilising their fields, while the remainder goes to a waste treatment plant, as normal. Research suggests that if bacteria in the plant's aeration tanks have even half as much nutrient-rich urine to deal with, it will take them a single day to munch all the nitrogen and phosphate matter instead of the usual thirty[*].

The Danes have followed suit. A farming collective near the town of Skibby operates a urine-separation project so successful that it is Denmark's largest producer of organic vegetables. Elsewhere Danish fruit-farmers are experimenting with spraying urine mixed with sulphur to prevent fungal diseases in blackcurrants.

In Finland, a bumper crop of experimental cabbages was fertilised with urine from private homes. Researchers said growth and biomass were higher than with conventional fertilizer, with no difference in nutritional value. As they hastened to assure people, the cabbages also smelled perfectly normal.

Beyond Scandinavia the revolution is spreading. The Swiss have experimented with extracting nitrogen and potassium in forms that

---

See: flushed[*]

can be sprayed directly on to crops. In the Netherlands phosphate is precipitated out as the mineral struvite (ammonium magnesium phosphate), which is not only a useful fertiliser but helps reduce the demand for mined phosphate. There are similar projects in Austria and Germany.

On the other side of the world, Australians were shocked to calculate that they excrete 25 million litres of urine every day and use 300 million litres of water to flush it away. They have initiated a three-year urine recycling trial in the award-winning eco-village at Currumbin on Queensland's Gold Coast. The same principles are being used in the world's poorer communities to save water and boost crop production, with South Africa, India, China and Mexico all starting to catch on.

Meanwhile the urine revolution is spreading to domestic gardens. The most daring gardeners now pee straight on to straw-bales or sawdust during the winter for composting. But even the modest are learning to save a little for flower-beds and vegetable plots. Since concentrated urine can deliver a nitrogen overload (witness the burned lawn at the spot where the family dog heads each morning), gardeners recommend diluting it in ten to twenty parts of water first.

With adults reckoned to produce roughly eleven grams of wasted nitrogen a day, more and more tillers of the soil are bringing urine in from the cold. The shoots of this eco-revolution are growing fast.

Electricity

PHYSICISTS IN SINGAPORE announced in 2005 that they had found a new way of generating electricity. The world listened, agog. It turned out to be a paper battery powered by urine.

The scientists at the Institute of Bioengineering and Nanotechnology created the credit card-sized battery as a disposable power source for medical test kits. They soaked a piece of paper in copper chloride and then sandwiched it between strips of magnesium and copper.

Urine contains ions (electrically charged atoms), which allow a chemical reaction to take place that in turn produces electricity. Dr Ki Bang Lee explained that with 0.2ml of urine, they were able to generate a voltage of around 1.5V with a corresponding maximum power of 1.5MW.

By the middle of 2007 rechargeable pee-powered batteries were on the shelves in Japan – deliciously marketed under the brand-name NoPoPo. You charge the NO POllution POwer battery by drawing up the urine with a tiny syringe and squeezing it into the battery. (The small print reveals that plain water will do just as well as urine to activate the charge, but that's obviously boring.)

When the urine is injected into an AA battery, the mixture of magnesium and carbon reacts to produce up to 500 milli-amp-hours of life, putting it on a par with zinc-carbon batteries but a long way behind alkaline ones with a life of up to 3000mAh. So, while electricity from urine is disposable and planet-friendly, there's probably no-po-point racing off to Japan just yet.

Enuresis

THE POSH NAME for bed-wetting. Amazingly, a European study has taken the trouble to establish that the nightly flow of urine from a seasoned bed-wetter can cost about $1,000 a year in laundry, sheets, disposable nappies and mattress replacement. Since this can carry on till the age of six for girls and seven for boys, so-called 'nocturnal enuresis' is an expensive business.

Enzyme Harvest

HARVESTING THE MULTITUDE of medically powerful ingredients in urine could become big business. Take urokinase, an enzyme originally isolated from urine by G.W. Sobel and then manufactured for use in dissolving the blood-clots that cause heart disease and strokes. Why not, it occurred to a small portable toilet company, get it straight from urine again? After all, they had an awful lot of pee passing through their portals.

Ironically, Porta John of America had started by looking for a way of getting rid of the smelly urine components in its toilets. But when they began consulting about a filtration system, scientists told them they were sitting on a goldmine. Get filtering, they were told. Only don't throw away what you trap.

Before long Porta John's toilets were reported to be collecting about four-and-a-half pounds of urokinase annually from the 14 million gallons of urine estimated to flow into them. Enough, it's been calculated, to unclog 260,000 coronary arteries. The more difficult job is selling it. Regulatory approval to market their brand, Tru-Kinase, has proved harder to secure than the enzymes.

But why stop at urokinase? Porta John joined forces with the Michigan biotech company Pharmaceuticals.org to work at retrieving some of the other enzymes in those millions of gallons of urine. Under the banner 'Pharmaceuticals from the Human System to the Human System', they offer a lengthy inventory of human-sourced proteins including albumin (a blood plasma protein used in manufactured form to restore failing circulation), growth hormone (which treats deficiencies of the same hormone), interferon (used to help the immune system fight cancer), collagen (a protein 'glue' used in burns and cosmetic surgery), insulin for diabetes, and endorphins for pain relief.

The company is seeking partnerships to extract these and others from portable toilets around the world and, once again, must secure the permission of regulators to market them for medical use.

The economic viability of this kind of enterprise has yet to be established. But with horse pee already supplying hormone replacement therapy[*] and the human variety boasting a long history as the saviour of infertile women[**] , there are successful precedents. Like the alchemists of old[***], businesses seem to believe there really is gold to be found in urine.

See: Neigh Oestrogen[*]
    Nuns[**]
    Alchemist's Reward[***]

Eternal Flame

CALLING A FLAME 'ETERNAL' is just inviting trouble. However dignified the memorial, however respectful that blazing symbol, somebody is always going to be tempted to put it out.

Since 1921 the eternal flame at the Tomb of the Unknown Soldier under the Arc de Triomphe in Paris had withstood storms and gales with scarcely a flicker. But at the end of June 1998 it took only a few seconds for a drunken World Cup football fan to douse it with a single fierce jet of pee.

Rodrigo Rafael Ortega from Mexico had been lolling around the Champs-Élysées with a supply of beer to extinguish the painful memories of being knocked out by Germany in the last sixteen. Taking careful aim, he extinguished the eternal flame while he was at it. The twenty-four-year-old was promptly arrested for being intoxicated in public and committing what the French authorities called 'an unspeakable act' against the nation's war dead. On 1 July a private ceremony was held to relight the flame, at which Mexico's ambassador to France, Sandra Fuentes-Berain, laid a wreath.

The Mexicans have their own eternal flame at the base of El Ángel de la Independencia in Mexico City, which honours the heroes of that country's War of Independence. This also receives the attention of incontinent football supporters from time to time. But, unlike Ortega's gesture in France, it is usually when Mexico has something to celebrate.

Back in Paris the eternal flame of remembrance burns on, disturbed only briefly by an Australian tourist who was arrested for trying to cook an egg over it.

Fighter Pilots

IT IS A DANGEROUS business trying to urinate in a fighter jet while flying solo at 800kph. An F-16 Fighting Falcon is reported to have crashed in Turkey that way in 1992. When the pilot tried to remove his safety strap to relieve himself, his belt buckle became wedged between the seat and the control stick.

It's also unwise to avoid liquids in the hope that the need won't arise: even a little dehydration can reduce a fighter pilot's ability to withstand heavy G-forces. Some pilots have been known to damage their bladders by holding on for hours.

The standard equipment has long been the 'piddle pack', a pistol-shaped plastic container filled with chemicals that converts urine into a gelatinous substance to be disposed of later; women pilots have their own version. That's all very well during a clear, daytime flight during the summer. But it doesn't make for an easy procedure when you're dressed in seven or eight layers for the cold.

As fighter jet pilot Col Phil Murdock, of the Vermont Air National Guard, puts it: 'Wintertime flying across the North Atlantic when you're wearing multiple thermal layers, or at night when you're trying to fly formation with other airplanes in rough weather, then it's darn near an emergency procedure.'

Now a new underwear system has been developed for fighter pilots. It comes with a hose linked to a pump the size of a paperback book that drains urine into a collection bag. The men's model uses a pouch and the women's is more like a sanitary towel. It means pilots of both sexes can navigate the plane, monitor weapons and watch out for mountains without struggling with the need to spend a penny. And for that, those of us on the ground should probably be grateful.

fire

IN 2007 FIRE-FIGHTERS in the Chinese province of Sichuan used urine to extinguish a blaze in two rural farmhouses in Chengdu. They had first tried pumping water from two wells in the village of Lianzing's, but these quickly ran dry as the fire raged on. That was when they spotted two large sewage tanks.

The fire-fighters found a way of pumping the urine out and then sprayed it successfully over the burning houses. Its 95% water content saved the day.

Reports insist, somewhat unconvincingly (since how can anyone possibly know), that this was the first time in history that a fire had been extinguished with urine. Of course, it's a record that doesn't take Gulliver's heroic efforts at Lilliput into account[*].

fizz

IT WAS PROBABLY only a matter of time before someone in India looked at the range of products made from sacred cow's urine – the soap, the aftershave, the toothpaste, the shampoo, the scented (yes) water – and wondered how it might taste with bubbles. Now the pee of the country's most sacred animal is being tipped to fly off the shelves as a fizzy drink. Bolstered by thousands of years of medicinal history[**], it's being developed by

See: Gulliver's Travels[*]
    Hinduism[**]

Hindu nationalists to take on the mighty Pepsi and Coca-Cola brands and further the cause of ridding India of foreign influences. You have to admire the *chutzpah*.

'Don't worry,' says Om Prakash, head of the Cow Protection Department of the nationalist Rashtriya Swayamsevak Sangh party. 'It won't smell like urine and will be tasty too.' To make it palatable we're told it will be mixed with aloe vera and gooseberry. Which might or might not help.

Not everyone is happy about the new drink, though. Another group of Hindus are already selling neat cow's urine from their temple thirty-five miles from the Taj Mahal, and sources suggest they are sniffy about the competition. They insist that only certain pure bred Indian cows are holy enough to produce the right kind of pee. Theirs is filtered and sold in 100ml bottles for 35 pence.

But Om Prakash believes the fizzy version of *gau jal* (cow water) will take India by storm. 'We may,' he added ominously, 'think of exporting it.'

flushed

FLUSHING URINE AWAY consumes such a breathtaking amount of water that you'd think waterless urinals and eco-toilets would be the obvious way ahead. But nobody told Philadelphia's plumbers. The city's powerful Plumbers' Union was aghast to discover that the 58-storey Comcast Center, the tallest skyscraper in Pennsylvania, was to be built with 116 environmentally sensitive urinals. No water, pointed out the union, meant fewer pipes. And fewer pipes meant less work for plumbers. Plugs, it was muttered darkly, might have to be pulled.

In vain the developers, Liberty Property Trust, protested that the urinals would be saving the city 1.6 million gallons of water a year and make the Comcast Center the tallest environmentally friendly building in the United States. The plumbers were unmoved. Eventually a compromise was reached by which pipes were installed 'just in case' water might be needed in the future. The tower opened gratefully in June 2008.

But as the employees of the Comcast cable corporation piddle happily in their 116 urinals, smug in the knowledge that their pee is being broken down by microbial spores rather than flushed away with precious water to a power-hungry treatment plant, the rest of us are left reflecting on the magnitude of waste elsewhere.

If the developer's calculations are correct, even a modest building with around forty urinals is pouring away enough water to fill an Olympic swimming pool every year. At home a full third of the water we use each day goes on flushing the toilet. At fourteen litres a flush with an older cistern, that's up to seventy litres a day. Even the newest toilets still use an average five litres of water per flush, making a massive 9,000 litres a year. And that water has already been treated to make it good enough to drink.

But it's not only water being wasted in our plumbing system. The chemical nutrients that could be isolated in eco-toilets and put to work in controlled quantities as fertiliser*are instead being expensively removed in sewage treatment plants. Despite making up only one per cent of waste-water, urine contributes about eighty per cent of the nitrogen and forty-five per cent of all the phosphate. If you flush it untreated into rivers and lakes, it could wreck the eco-system by over-fertilising aquatic plants, which will use up oxygen in the water and so suffocate the fish.

But converting it into harmless biomass in treatment plants takes enormous amounts of energy. The UK uses 65,000 gigajoules a day to pump, stir, heat and aerate our urine – that's about a quarter of the output of the country's largest coal-fired power station.

All over the world we are flushing energy, water and precious soil-nutrients down the pan. Perhaps the plumbers of Pennsylvania are not the only ones who need to readjust their priorities.

See: Eco Revolution*

forgery

THE WORLD'S MOST accomplished counterfeiter knew how to make fake coins look so authentic that they could fool Europe's greatest museums and collectors. Carl Wilhelm Becker became such a celebrated forger that some of his counterfeits are now worth more than the originals. His secret was urine.

To achieve the worn and weathered look of well-circulated coins, this son of a German vintner put his forgeries in a bucket of earth hung from the axle of a cart which he bumped along the Continent's cobbled roads. After that he buried the coins in a shallow hole and sprinkled them liberally with urine.

Becker, who was born in the German town of Speyer in 1772, was fastidious about using the right kind of pee. He claimed the rich morning variety was better than anything produced in the afternoon. He reckoned that a woman's urine turned bronze a different shade of green to a man's[*]. And like the old woollen workers[**], he was convinced that the urine of a beer drinker offered a different quality of patina from someone who preferred wine.

Becker's habit was to water his cache of coins a couple times a day for a week or two, and then dig them up after a month. Silver coins would have turned grey or black and bronze coins could range from chocolate brown to avocado green.

Becker worked within a long, if not entirely honourable, tradition of using urine in the production of fake coins and medals. The Romans were at it, for certain. In 2003 academics from the University of Rome examined a silver coin minted in the third century BC and realised that some enterprising Roman counterfeiter had dissolved silver chloride in urine and then coated a worthless lump of lead with it.

Today rubbing urine into fake pieces of art to dull the shine is still common in China, acknowledged as the world capital of counterfeiting. Forgers of Nazi memorabilia also find that soaking

See: 𝔓icasso[*]
    𝔇ye[**]

their counterfeit daggers and pin badges in pee does the trick like nothing else.

A recipe for modern forgers to cook up that authentic patina makes it sound all too easy:

> Place two cups of forged coins into a small lapidary rock tumbler.
> Add 1 tablespoon of pea-gravel and a quarter cup of very fine dirt.
> Add an optional pinch of sulphur.
> Finish by adding three cups of unrefined liquid uric acid.[11]

For just the right variety of 'unrefined liquid uric acid', you would have to consult a master pee forger like Carl Wilhelm Becker.

frostbite

PEEING IN SUB-ZERO temperatures has to be fast. When temperatures are low enough to freeze living tissue, every exposed etremity is at risk – as a young man in Stavropol was horrified to discover in the notorious Russian winter of 2003. Normally one of the warmer regions, Stavropol hit a low of minus 30 degrees centigrade that January. Nobody was prepared for it, least of all the tipsy lad who decided to relieve himself beside a bus shelter on his way home from a bar.

Swaying a little as he got down to business, the youth suddenly found himself stuck fast to the frozen metal. A gaping crowd gathered and began to shout helpful suggestions, none of which solved his excruciating – and increasingly dangerous – plight. Eventually he was freed with the aid of a kettle of warm water borrowed from a nearby chemist's shop. Once liberated, the victim ran away before anyone could check whether he had become one of the ten per cent of frostbite cases that involve the ears, nose, cheeks or penis.

frozen

THE URBAN MYTH that there are frozen icicles of urine flying through our skies every day, threatening to lance hapless citizens through the heart, masks an only slightly less disconcerting truth. Frozen urine does indeed fall occasionally from planes, it seems. And people have almost been hit.

- In 2003 Canadian Chris Hastings was woken by a large crash outside his home in Manitoba. He emerged to find 'a basketball-sized chunk of yellowish ice' on the roof of his blue estate car.
- In February 2008 a gang of builders in the village of North Stifford in Essex claimed to have come within inches of being killed by a similarly suspicious missile from a passing plane. This one was 'football-sized'.
- A few months later another part of Essex was under attack from a 20kg lump of 'frozen toilet waste', which landed at the feet of shop assistant Joanne Bojas in Chelmsford. 'If it had hit me on the head I would have been killed,' she told reporters.
- In Austria a couple sought legal redress in June 2009, when a block of what was allegedly frozen urine smashed through the roof of their house in Hartbert. Hans and Irene Schüler demanded details of flight movements, so that they could claim compensation from the airline responsible.
- A mysteriously damaged wind turbine in Lincolnshire in January 2009 prompted speculation that frozen urine could be to blame. It was thought somewhat more likely than a UFO-strike.

The authorities concede that these things do happen. The UK's Civil Aviation Authority admitted to thirty-five reported cases of falling ice in 2009 – a tiny percentage of some 3 million flights, though not much consolation if you find yourself under one of them. It's impossible to tell how many of these icy missiles would have contained urine. The ice forms from water leaking from the aircraft – possibly, though not necessarily, from the toilets. It seeps out of the plane, freezes quickly at the sub-zero temperatures up there, breaks off as ice and plummets to the earth. It often, but not always, thaws on its way down.

However, we are assured that nothing is deliberately dumped. 'Toilets are not emptied until the plane is grounded,' says the CAA firmly, adding that in forty years there have been just five cases of people being hit.

fullers, Tuckers and Walkers

FULLERS, TUCKERS AND Walkers bear the names of a lost craft. They are the dying whisper of a forgotten industrial tradition and a trade that no longer dares speak its name.

Urine was for hundreds of years a core component in Britain's booming woollen industry – and indeed across Europe. It was saved and collected, solicited and donated, bought and sold in every cloth-producing area of the country. Its vital role was commemorated in the surnames of the men who did the work of *fulling*, or cleaning, fabric – a craft also known as *walking* and *tucking* (done in Wales by the *twcwr*). *Waulking* in Scotland and *walking* in parts of England referred originally to beating or kneading the cloth by hand to make it shrink and thicken. Urine was a key element in both the scouring and the thickening.

From medieval times the fuller's practice was to climb into a knee-deep barrel of urine and jump up and down on the cloth to clean it. This was the 'fuller's leap' described by Seneca hundreds of years earlier*. It worked the alkaline ammonia into the fabric, literally stamping out any oiliness and grime still clinging to the wool. Urine was then used as a thickening agent to help matt the fibres further**.

Gradually small water-powered fulling mills took over the pounding of the cloth from human legs, with two enormous hammers beating down on the urine-soaked fabric to loosen the grease. Those mills were found all over Europe. In Spain Cervantes had his eponymous Don Quixote spend a hilarious night with

---

See: Romans*
     Harris Tweed**

Sancho Panza in terror at their deafening thud: 'Six huge fulling-mill hammers which interchangeably thumping several pieces of cloth, made the terrible noise that caus'd all Don Quixote's anxieties and Sancho's tribulation that night.'

Remarkably, the throb of wooden hammers beating cloth in troughs of old pee continued in parts of Britain until the 1930s. Families often rallied round to help finish the cloth. Pre-industrial cottage weavers in the West Riding of Yorkshire collected what was known as 'wash' from everybody in the household in large pots, and scoured their completed cloth in it themselves. But professional fullers, tuckers and walkers needed more urine than even the biggest family could provide. They paid for household urine by the bucket, collected by horse-drawn cart from local homes.

Generations of families in wool-processing areas supplemented their income by supplying a bucket or two every day for the fulling mills, with double pay in some parts if you were a Methodist*. A delightful indigenous vocabulary also developed to describe the service. The horse that clopped around the Huddersfield village of Thurstonland collecting stale pee (known there as *weeting*) rejoiced in the name of the *weetin-dob*.

Urine was still being bought by the bucket-load as late as the 1930s. In north Yorkshire the local collector was known – affectionately one hopes – as Piss Willie. It's true the name doesn't ring with the distinction of Fuller, Tucker or Walker, but like the generic Seck-Hannes (Piss Hans) doing the same job in Germany, Piss Willie was an indispensable link in the textile chain that kept economies thriving and people in clothes for a very long time.

See: 𝔥andy 𝔓andy*

Gas Masks

AT SUNRISE ON 22 April 1915, French soldiers on the front at Ypres in Belgium noticed yellow-green clouds drifting towards them. The clouds spread out across four miles of trench lines, making the air smell of something survivors later struggled to describe. Someone made a stab at pineapple mixed with pepper. If those men had ever been in a modern swimming pool, they would have recognised the smell of chlorine.

Within ten minutes of the gas reaching them, 5,000 men were dead, choked by noxious fumes. Those who lived were temporarily blinded and stumbled around in such confusion that 2,000 of them were captured. The German army had released 5,700 canisters containing 168 tons of chlorine gas.

Two days later Canadian troops north-east of Ypres saw a second gas cloud approaching. But this time they had an unlikely defence to hand. An order attributed to Captain Francis Scrimger, medical officer with the 2nd Canadian Field Ambulance, was relayed around the trenches. Each man was to urinate immediately on his handkerchief, place it over nose and mouth to form a pad and breath through it.

As the gas drifted inexorably towards them, it's not hard to imagine the fumbling panic of the soldiers' struggle to comply. But this early gas mask may well have made the difference between life and death for some of them.

What Captain Scrimger must have understood is that chlorine is slightly soluble in water. It had also been known since 1908 that it would react with urea to form dichloro-urea.[12] The urea thus 'absorbed' the chlorine, reducing the amount of toxic gas that could enter the lungs and cause the damage.

Professor Alan Dronsfield, chair of the Royal Society of Chemistry's Historical Group, says that although the concentration of urea in urine is too low to have had a dramatic effect, the advice to the troops was sound: 'The protection would have been limited, though better than nothing.'

Within days Allied troops were issued with cloth pads sewn by local Frenchwomen. They were given instructions to dampen them with a sodium bicarbonate solution, kept specially in buckets for the purpose, which would absorb the chlorine in the same way as urine.

By July of 1915 the entire British army had been equipped with 'smoke helmets' covering the whole head, which gave soldiers much more effective protection from gas attack. It was urine, though, that deserves the credit for seeing them through at the beginning.

Gender-Bender

URINE IS NOT the stuff of many fantasies that can be mentioned in polite society, but it does encourage one. Once we have bidden our pee a hasty farewell, we like to think it whooshes off never to be seen again. Sadly, the reality is different. Our urine footprint never goes away.

What urine actually does is head for our rivers, where, frankly, it gets up to no good. Nutrients like nitrogen and phosphorus have to be removed expensively at waste treatment plants along the way, otherwise they over-fertilise aquatic plants and starve fish of oxygen*. Meanwhile traces of all the synthetic chemicals we have

---

See: flushed*

consumed, both from medications and recreational drugs[*], continue on their way untreated. Some are implicated in changing the sex of fish. It's believed that some may even bid us a cheery hello again, as they re-appear from the kitchen tap.

For instance, British water quality scientists have reported a 'high probability' that cytotoxic chemotherapy drugs, the most poisonous class of pharmaceuticals, are present at concentrations of a few nanograms per litre in river water.[13] These are the drugs designed to kill the rapidly growing cells of a tumour. A wonderful boon to cancer sufferers, their disruptive action on DNA replication means they can harm most living things. The scientists note a 'theoretical risk' that in the parts of the UK where river-water downstream of a waste treatment works is recycled for drinking-water, some traces may slip through the purification processes to return to our taps.[14]

The scientists, based at the Centre for Ecology and Hydrology at Wallingford in Oxfordshire, add: 'It is highly unlikely that concentrations below the nanograms per litre level would represent a risk to adults. However, the developing human embryo inside a pregnant woman could be particularly vulnerable to minute amounts of these agents, as they would be able to pass through the gut and placenta.'

There are a lot of alarmist 'could's, and 'might's, and 'theoretical's, in the science of chemical residues in rivers, and not all scientists are convinced. The most securely established link is between the contraceptive pill and 'feminised' male fish. Studies for the Environment Agency suggest a firm cause and effect between female sex hormones (and the chemicals that mimic these oestrogens) and extensive gender-bending in male roach which has left some of them unable to produce sperm.

A more recent study suggests that testosterone-blocking chemicals known as anti-androgens, which have been found in thirty rivers across England, might not only be feminising fish but playing a part in feminising men.[15] Male fertility has been declining

---

See: Cocaine[*]

for the last fifty years and it's argued that recycled anti-androgens could be contributing. Professor Charles Tyler, of the University of Exeter, says studies on rats and mice have shown that even a small amount of anti-androgens found in several medicines could affect male fertility in mammals.

All this is theory rather than fact. But even the disputes among scientists emphasise how little anyone really knows about the ultimate fate of the chemical load carried by urine. We are always being advised not to flush drugs down the toilet. The trouble is we do, all the time, without giving it a second thought.

George III

AS IF IT'S not bad enough to go down in history for losing the American colonies and mistaking a large tree for the king of Prussia, George III bears another burden. He is remembered for producing extraordinary urine. During his many long and severe bouts of insanity, the royal wee was minutely observed, giving later researchers a field day as they tried to work out what exactly was ailing Britain's third Hanoverian monarch.

At the age of 50 the king first experienced abdominal pain and constipation, followed by weak limbs, fever, a fast pulse and hoarseness. His urine was dark red. Combined with delirium, convulsions and a propensity for ripping off his wig and running about naked, the symptoms convinced people that the king was mad.

But twentieth-century researchers suggested that the red urine was caused by the rare metabolic disease porphyria (from the Greek for purple pigment), in which the blood pigment haemoglobin is not made properly. Excess porphyrins are formed, red in colour, which are then excreted in the urine. The condition can cause mental problems and personality changes.

George III recovered from this first bout of porphyria but relapsed later, when his urine had more surprises in store. In January 1811, when he was again dangerously ill and so mentally unstable that his eldest son was about to take over as Prince Regent, his physician, Sir Henry Halford, reported a bizarre development:

'The water is of a deeper colour,' he wrote, 'and leaves a pale blue ring upon the glass near the upper surface.'

Blue urine has been linked to the biochemical conversion of certain foods into indigo. In 1901 physicians treating a patient by the name of John Good reported that his was 'peacock blue'. They put this down to 'the formation of indigo through oxidation of the indican that results from the putrefactive activity of the Bacillus coli upon the products of tryptic digestion'[16] – which to the rest of us means that poor John Good was so badly constipated that some nasty stuff made it into the bloodstream and out via his urine.

It's good to have Mr Good's peacock-blue pee sorted out. But since nobody seems to have established a link between indigo in urine and mental instability, the mystery of King George's madness continues.

Golfers

It's not everyone who would spare a thought for golfers taken short at the third hole, with the club-house far behind and not a bush in sight. But Floyd E. Seskin, MD, is on their side. Spotting a gap in the market for players who just can't wait any longer, the enterprising Florida urologist developed the UroClub – a portable urinal shaped like a seven-iron, which has been hollowed inside to accommodate half a litre of pee.

Dr Seskin says he was inspired by patients suffering from urinary frequency, although one assumes the $50 price tag was inspirational too. Best of all, the UroClub comes with a cheeky towel that you clip to your waistband like an apron and drape casually over the fake iron. Then you fiddle about behind it, unscrewing the triple-sealed, leak-proof cap and aiming (blind) into the club while remarking pleasantly on the weather in a manner that suggests it is perfectly normal to wear a towel on a golf course. 'It's the only club in your bag guaranteed to keep you out of the woods,' Dr Seskin assures us pithily.

But there's worse. Another American company is offering putting practice for golfers who want to hone their skills while seated on the toilet with trousers at half-mast. This is not normally considered an ideal golfing position, but the Potty Putter comes complete with a miniature putting green to spread around your feet, a doughnut-shaped hole marked by a cheeky flag, and a thoughtful *Do Not Disturb* notice for the bathroom door.

Anyone so seriously incompetent that they need practice at a range of 12 inches should consider the problems of ball retrieval.

Gulliver's Travels

WHEN AN ACCOUNT of the adventures of Lemuel Gulliver was released in two volumes in 1726, it became an instant bestseller. The book is a caustic satire on the human condition but Jonathan Swift also used his artless hero to take some personal swipes at his enemies. In particular, Gulliver's well-meaning peeing on a fire in the dinky Lilliputlian palace allowed Swift a sly dig at his *bête noire*, Queen Anne.

When Lilliput's tiny but self-important worthies badger Gulliver for assistance in putting out the fire in the empress's five foot-high royal apartments, he records that an evening of wine-drinking has set him up perfectly for the task: 'The heat I had contracted by coming very near the flames, and by labouring to quench them, made the wine begin to operate my urine; which I voided in such a quantity, and applied so well to the proper places, that in three minutes the fire was wholly extinguished.'

The empress, however, is too outraged by the desecration of her miniscule apartments to appreciate the rescue. Instead, for one of literature's more thankless urinations Gulliver is sentenced to have his eyes put out with arrows.

The scene has added piquancy when you realise that the empress was probably intended to represent Queen Anne, and that the pint-sized royal's disgust may have been linked to Anne's well-attested dislike of Swift's work and her attempts to limit his prospects in the Church of England. Revenge is sweet.

Gunpowder

IT MUST HAVE been distressing to live at a time when gunpowder was made from a substance in search of which complete strangers had the right to dig up your home. 'The saltpetre men care not in whose houses they dig,' raged Sir Francis Seymour in 1630, 'threatening men that by their commission they may dig in any man's house, in any room, and at any time, which will prove a great grievance to the country.'

It was indeed an enormous grievance to citizens in many countries that the chief ingredient in gunpowder was obtained from barnyards, stables, cellars, pigeon lofts and the earthen floors of their houses. Potassium nitrate, known as saltpetre (from the Latin *sal petrae*, salt of rock), was formed primarily from the action of animal urine on soil. Carted away by the infamous 'petremen', the rotting muck was then refined in wood-ash and lime and kept moist with more urine; bacteria helped convert the ammonium to nitrates. Ultimately the release of oxygen from saltpetre would promote the rapid burning of gunpowder's other ingredients, sulphur and charcoal, to produce an explosion[*].

It was, of course, the poor who had their homes damaged and carts requisitioned to carry raw saltpetre away. Teams of petremen plunged into houses, sick-rooms and churches, regardless of who was in them and with airy disregard to foundations and walls. Francis Seymour, a younger brother of the 2nd Duke of Somerset, told Charles I's secretary of state Sir John Coke: 'If any oppose them they break up men's houses and dig by force. They make men carry their saltpetre at a groat a mile, and take their carriages in sowing time and harvest, with many other oppressions.'[17]

The king himself was flooded with petitions, both *about* the abuses of the petremen and *by* the hated collectors themselves who found, as one Thomas Thornhill complained in 1631, that citizens were thwarting them by paving their cellars with stone or filling them with gravel. Recognising the problems, the king was tempted

---

See: **Confederate Belles**[*]

by a proposed new method of simply collecting neat human urine and mixing it with soil. The entrepreneur behind the idea, Thomas Russell, told him that if 10,000 villages, each with forty houses occupied by four persons, all cast their urine on a load of earth for three months and then let it rest for three months longer, ripe saltpetre would result.

Charles granted Russell and Sir John Brooke a patent in 1625 to try out the idea, and in an extraordinary royal dictate duly ordered his long-suffering subjects to 'keep and preserve in some convenient vessels or receptacles fit for the purpose, all the urine of man during the whole year'. While they were at it, their animals' urine was to be collected too.

But peeing for England's wars raised little enthusiasm. The new system flopped and the old search-and-find methods continued, with occasional legislative attempts to restrain the excesses. The Civil War between Charles and his parliament eventually strained England's supplies of gunpowder so much that the hunt for saltpetre had to be stepped up. When the Lords and Commons ordered more production in 1644 to boost depleted Roundhead stores, they also ordained that the freshly unleashed saltpetremen had to make good any damage at their own expense.

It was only in 1656, with Cromwell's Protectorate busy promoting peace, that petremen were at last forbidden to dig in houses or lands without permission of the owner to search for urine.

Gypsy Moth

IN JULY 1935 a British expedition to Mount Everest found the body of a climber at the foot of the North Col. It was wrapped in the weather-shredded remains of a tent, with a rucksack close by containing a diary. The concluding entry was dated 31 May 1934 and read simply: 'Off again, gorgeous day.'

The artless enthusiasm of Maurice Wilson's final message poignantly summed up the man who had piloted himself out to India for his attempt on the world's highest peak in a Gypsy Moth plane after only two months flying experience. He then prepared for the ascent by fasting on water and urine alone. Regular ingestion of pee plus the power of God could achieve anything, he believed.

Wilson was a mill worker's son from Bradford and a decorated First World War hero. Convinced that prayer and urine-fasting would enable him to succeed where George Mallory had failed, he originally planned to crash-land his Gypsy Moth (which he named Ever Wrest) onto the upper slopes of Everest and then walk to the summit. But his plane was impounded in India, so he hiked overland through forbidden Tibet instead, disguised as a Buddhist monk. Eventually he set off from base camp with the frozen food remains from the large British expedition of 1933 and a shaving mirror to signal to monks at the Rongbuk monastery fifteen miles away. It was a suicidal mission.

Wilson believed his frequent bouts of fasting on water and urine* had given him a stamina that would stand him in good stead for the rigours to come. It's a practice he may have picked up from a group of Indian *amaroli* enthusiasts** whom he had met earlier on a ship home from New Zealand, or from the Tibetan llamas he spent time with before his attempt on Everest.

The llamas are reputed to owe their famed longevity to drinking the urine of superior or elevated llamas, whose purity of mind is supposed to be reflected in the purity of their bodily secretions. Wilson is also reported to have massaged urine into his skin, as advocated by the llamas, for enhanced vigour and energy.

Alas, no amount of enhanced vigour, robust stamina, reckless bravery or indomitable faith could compensate for Maurice Wilson's alarming inexperience in glacier climbing. He made several attempts at the summit in May 1934 but was beaten in the end, probably by exhaustion. One of his last diary entries, on 28 May, captured a naive optimism and a confidence so sunny that you begin to understand why he felt he could pull off the most daunting

---

See: 𝔇rinking 𝔍t*
     𝔥induism**

LIFE OF ＰEE

mountain on earth without training, equipment or clothing. 'This
will be a last effort,' he wrote, 'and I feel successful.'

The members of Eric Shipton's expedition found him the
following year in the snow, lying on his left side with his knees
drawn up, wearing just a mauve pullover and grey flannel trousers
over a woollen vest and pants. They buried him in a nearby crevasse.
As the body of this endearingly foolhardy Englishman slid into the
depths, his countrymen raised their hats.

ħanðy Þanðy

IT CERTAINLY PAID to be a Methodist in parts of rural Wales. Not only was heaven within your grasp, so was a premium-rate income from your pee.

The man running the local fulling-mill, or *pandy* in Welsh, needed large quantities of urine to clean the cloth sent there by local weavers. So he bought it in, driving his horse and cart around the houses of his regular customers each day, collecting their pails of household urine, emptying these into a cask on the wagon and handing over payment. In the nineteenth century the going rate for a bucket of urine was one penny. Methodists, enjoying an extra perk of righteousness, could make twice as much.

We cannot be certain why Methodists' pee was worth twopence a bucket to some Welsh fullers. Was it because tea, the favourite tipple of abstemious chapel-goers, is less acidic than alcohol (unless it's taken very black) and more likely to boost the alkaline properties of the urine? Or was it that Methodists might be expected to eat less rich food? The celebrated nineteenth-century dyer William Partridge certainly thought urine from 'persons living on plain diet' was stronger and better than that from 'luxurious livers' – presumably because a high-protein diet is again more acidic[*].

The records are largely silent on the details of this trade but the price differential may well have begun at the time of the powerful Methodist revival in the eighteenth century, which filled Welsh chapels with eager new Christians. Perhaps the fullers began to notice an improvement in the quality of urine as the lifestyles of the converted changed, and used market forces to encourage the teetotallers. There might even have been fullers of an evangelical bent who thought it no bad thing to offer a financial incentive to bolster conversion or discourage backsliding. Whatever the reason, fullers in Wales thought it worth offering a reward for salvation.

Wales was generously sprinkled with those small waterwheel-powered fulling mills. As many as 400 place-names with *pandy* in them have been found on old maps, including the one made famous by the former Speaker of the House of Commons, Lord Tonypandy. Each one recalls the site of a mill in which urine was used to finish cloth.

At one time there were as many as three *pandai* in the village of Dre-fach Felindre in Carmarthenshire alone, serving an astonishing 24 woollen mills within one square mile of the village. Now one of those mills is the site of the engaging National Wool Museum. It's there you will find the last remnant of the urine trade in the Welsh valleys: a fuller's tin bucket, a battered, dirty thing, its insides thickened and pocked with the orangey-black encrustations of generations of pee. The fuller (Welsh *twcwr*) would have used it to decant the household urine into a large tub. Here the woven cloth was soaked to remove grease, before being pounded clean by two mighty fulling hammers driven by the water-powered wheel outside[**].

Buckets like this were used in the *pandai* of Wales for 600 years, from as early as 1330 right through to the 1930s, when the last one closed. Although the tradition is largely forgotten now, the language

---

See: 𝔇ye[*]

𝔣ullers, 𝔗uckers and 𝔚alkers[**]

remembers. There is an unflattering Welsh expression, *hanner pan*, which suggests that someone is 'not quite there'. What it literally means is 'half-fulled'. The metaphor is of a person washed in urine that has not entirely done its job.

At the National Wool Museum Keith Rees, craftsman and tour guide, taps the one remaining crusty old bucket with his toe. 'I'm still waiting for someone to honour the tradition by donating,' he muses. 'I'm offering 10p but there have been no takers.' He strokes a grizzled beard and murmurs thoughtfully: 'Maybe I need to offer 20p to Methodists.'

ḣarris Cweeḋ

THE LAST WORKING pee-tub on the Hebridean island of Harris was in operation until the eve of the twenty-first century. It stood outside a modest house in the hamlet of Plockropool at the end of a shimmering, sea-girt road which (for reasons sadly unconnected) locals call the Golden Road. There weaver Marion Campbell made Harris tweeds the way her ancestors had always done – with local wool, natural dyes and copious quantities of household urine – until shortly before she died in 1996 at the age of 86.

Handmade Harris plaids had provided an income for islanders like Marion for generations. Wind-defying, hard-wearing and with a macho, man-in-the-heather charm, they made a popular uniform for upper-class gentlemen in the House of Lords, where the *je ne sais quoi* odour of wool and urine proclaimed the authentic brand. The whiff of real Harris Tweed was not unpleasant – nostalgic weavers describe it as 'lovely' – although it had an added pungency on humid days.

Central to the cottage industry on Harris was what they called the 'pee-tub', a big iron-lidded wooden barrel into which family chamber pots were emptied daily. Contributions from visitors were warmly accepted.

Sisters Katie Campbell and Ina Morrison, from a family of tweed-makers, still remember the range of uses to which that urine was put. First it helped to fix dye-colours to the sheep-fleeces: colours like the rich brown from *crotal*, a crumbly, greyish-black lichen that women scraped off the rocks with a spoon. The fleeces were laid in a huge black dye-pot between layers of crotal, like a trifle, with cold water and urine from the pee-tub poured on top. The mixture was then heated over a fire for three hours. On other fleeces they used heather, dandelions, irises for greens, the delicate light gold of onion skins or the subtle browns of peat soot and seaweed.

For blue they turned to imported indigo, using urine to stimulate the pigment itself. A muslin bag of indigo was put into a bucket of urine and left to warm at the hearth for three days, gently spilling its colour[*]. The sisters cheerfully ate their tea with a pail of pee steaming at the fireside.

Once the fleeces had been dyed and dried, the fibres carded and spun into yarn, and then all the different shades of yarn woven into tweed, came the process known in Scotland as *waulking*[**]. Out came more urine, so that the ammonia could remove residual oiliness from the fabric and shrink it. At the safe distance of the barn, the woven tweed was soaked in a thigh-high barrel of urine and children were enlisted to stamp up and down on it, like the Roman fullers of old[***].

'We would add a bit of water and melted green Sunlight soap,' Ina remembers dreamily. 'Then we girls stepped into the tub with our welly-boots and trampled it. There would be thirty to forty yards of tweed and we'd stamp on it, going round and round. We called it "the stamping"'.

The tweed was then removed from the barrel, squeezed and laid across a piece of wood or corrugated iron stretched across a couple of chairs in the house. Two or three women sat at each side, singing Gaelic hymns as they beat it to the rhythm of the waulking songs, until the cloth had shrunk to exactly 29 inches, measured with a middle finger. If the tweed dried up, the girls would use their

---

See: Indigo[*]
      Fullers, Tuckers and Walkers[**]
      Romans[***]

fingers to sprinkle it with more pee from a jug. It was the last stage in urine's multi-purpose contribution to the making of traditional Harris Tweed.

The beginning of the end of the Harris pee-tub came about after an almighty battle between some estate-workers and their landlord, provoked by the crofters' attempt to plant grain illegally in his fields. The landlord managed to drive the men away, but their wives retaliated by raiding the pee-tubs and passing buckets of stale urine from hand to hand until they reached the landowner, making his lone stand in the field. The last woman in line launched the missile. Soaking wet and with smarting eyes, the wretched man was forced to retreat. But, as Harrisman Finlay J. Macdonald recalls in *Crowdie and Cream*, it was a pyrrhic victory for the islanders: the pee-tubs were so depleted in the course of the battle that there was an acute shortage of matured urine for tweed-making on Harris that year. An enterprising shopkeeper cashed in by importing bottled ammonia for the first time.

Yet some outposts of traditional tweed-making remained. At the end of the Golden Road at Plockropool, Katie Campbell's aunt by marriage, Marion Campbell, a formidably talented weaver, saw no reason to abandon the old ways, even if it was difficult to keep the pee-tub replenished.

'When her brothers died, Marion would run short of urine,' Katie recalls. 'She'd come round here and say in the Gaelic, "I need some *maistir*."' Katie shakes her iron curls and allows herself a fleetingly sheepish grin. 'Right to the end I'd go off and get the chamber pot and do what I could to help.'

Hindiusm

INDIAN RELIGION HAS always gone big, as it were, on wee. The Damar Tantra, a 5,000-year-old Sanskrit text, contains a full 107 stanzas on the benefits of drinking urine, or 'the water of the god Shiva'. Not only will all ailments be cured, it assures us, but old age itself will be banished.

This is not a document to value understatement. 'Nine years of this method will make the follower immortal ... After ten years it will be possible to float in the air with ease … Twelve years will enable one to live as long as the moon and the planets.' This is heady stuff.

In the Indian ayurvedic tradition the practice is called *amaroli*. One of the most famous devotees was the former Indian Prime Minister Morarji Desai, who lived to the impressive age of ninety-nine and blithely attributed his longevity to drinking his morning urine – a revelation that gave the CBS anchorman Dan Rather something of a turn when he was interviewing him. Desai was politically brazen enough to suggest that it was the perfect solution for Indians unable to afford medical care[*].

Hindus who balk at using their own urine can always turn to their most sacred animal instead. Cow's urine is marketed in every conceivable form of potion, lotion and pill. The devout will find it bottled as shampoo, aftershave and even as a sparkling drink[**].

Admittedly cow's urine has been submitted to tests that suggest the old Hindu tets, hyperbolic as they were, might have been on to something. Among these was a double-blind trial in 2003, in which fifty White Leghorn hens were given a disease vaccine and half of them then treated with 1ml of cow's urine. The results showed that the bovine urine had had a 'significant effect' on the immune status of the birds that received it.

ℌoward ℌughes

AMONG THE MORE eccentric habits adopted by the world's richest man as he descended into mental illness was storing his urine in milk bottles. These he labelled, dated and placed under the solicitous care of an assistant.

The once brilliant American aviator, industrialist, film producer and philanthropist began to show signs of obsessive-compulsive disorder in the 1930s, when friends noticed he was becoming fixated with the dimensions of the peas on his plate: he began arranging them by size with a special fork.

See: 𝔇rinking 𝔦t[*]
       𝔉izz[**]

By 1947 Howard Hughes was becoming so reclusive that he retreated to a film studio near his home for four months, where he watched film after film in the dark, naked, while stacking and restacking boxes of Kleenex tissues. He ate chocolate and drank milk, which helped when it came to finding bottles to store his jealously hoarded urine. His aides had strict instructions not to look at him or speak to him. He finally emerged in the spring of 1948, in need of a good wash.

Hydrogen fuel

POWERING CARS WITH hydrogen is increasingly attractive as a green transport option because the only emission is water, but where do you find a cheap, renewable source of hydrogen? It might be the most abundant element in the universe, but on earth it gets locked away in molecules like H_2O. Water itself is no good, because hydrogen can only be liberated if an electric current is passed through it – a prohibitively expensive process. Step forward, then, urine.

A team of scientists at Ohio University realised that the urea in urine incorporates four hydrogen atoms per molecule, which are less tightly bonded than the hydrogen atoms in water molecules. They found a way of producing hydrogen from urine using electrolysis, at a fraction of the cost of splitting water.

The team initially tested their process with synthetic urine made of dissolved urea, but after a long wait for clearance to work with human urine, they proved that the real thing worked a treat. They reckon the process could easily be scaled up to generate hydrogen while cleaning up the effluent from sewage plants.

The pee-powered car may not be far away.

Icelandic Shark

NO ICELANDIC SAGA is more terrifying than the story of how Icelanders pee on their national dish. 'But of course we urinate on shark-meat,' they assure wide-eyed tourists who have just speared a cube of pale, fleshy meat and are gagging at the stink of sour urine. 'How otherwise could it smell so much like one of your gentlemen's toilets?'

In truth some Icelanders, many of whom actually like the taste of *hákarl*, have almost convinced themselves. They wonder if it could possibly be true that before being buried in the earth for several weeks, their prime culinary delicacy is sent on its way underground with a generous splash of urine.

The man to settle the question is a former fisherman in Iceland's north-west fjords. Locals tell you there is nothing Finnbogi Bernódusson does not know about sharks. Dressed head to toe in antique oilskins, he can be found entertaining visitors among the tackle huts and drying racks of a charmingly reconstructed fishing station at Bolungarvík. Shark hunting was once a mainstay of the economy here, in the days when one shark's liver could produce up to 500 barrels of oil to light the street lamps of Europe.

Finnbogi strokes his cotton-grass beard and asks for questions. OK, then, Finnbogi. Here's one. Do Icelanders pee on the shark-meat before it's buried?

He looks pained. '*Nei, nei, nei,*' he protests, shaking his head so vigorously that the white hair lifts to a mesmerizing Mohican peak. 'I swear not. No pissing.'

What, none?

'Of course not,' Finnbogi glares. 'This story comes only because the smell is so bad. And the smell is bad because of the shark's ammonia.'

Sharks, it turns out, don't have a urinary tract, so they concentrate urea in their blood and excrete it through their skin. That makes the flesh of species like the Greenland shark, caught in Iceland, poisonous. If you eat it fresh, it produces effects similar to extreme drunkenness, which can be fatal. (In Greenland ' shark-sick' is still a euphemism for being drunk.)

But hungry Icelanders discovered centuries ago that burying the meat in the ground for several months, and then hanging it to get rid of ammonia and bacteria, makes shark perfectly safe to eat. It can hang for years, say connoisseurs, and mature like a fine Scotch.

The story goes that the discovery was first made around 1600, when the men of Asparvík in the north fed a dish of putrefied *hákarl* to some government busybodies with the sole purpose of finishing them off. They were amazed instead to find the guests all inconveniently thriving. A national dish was born.

SHARK CUISINE

Locate a dead shark.
>Cut into strips of meat 10 to 12 cm thick and 30 to 50 cm long.
>Put the strips into a hole in the ground 1.3 metres deep, with the meaty sides facing each other. Pile rocks on top and leave for up to 3 months to ferment.
>Dig the strips up and hang for 4 to 6 months till a brown shiny crust is formed.

Cut into cubes and serve as hors d'oeuvres at up-market parties and
   national feasts.
Ignore the smell.
Consume with a glass of fiery alcoholic brennivín (schnapps) to
   burn away the taste.
Congratulate yourself on an act of heroism.
Make a mental note never, ever to do it again.

Icy Noctiluca

IN 1677 AN extraordinary performance took place at the London
home of the scientist Robert Boyle, one of the founders of modern
chemistry. Daniel Kraft was in town, an alchemist famous for
demonstrating the wonders of phosphorus. The evening would lead
Boyle to extract this miraculous, glow-in-the-dark substance from
his own urine and give it the beautiful name Icy Noctiluca. From
it he produced the world's first striking match.

Boyle had invited Kraft to put on a display for the fellows of the
Royal Society of London, and the German gave them a terrific
performance. In the darkened room he passed around a bottle
containing a small piece of phosphorus. Boyle wrote later that it
glowed at first 'like a cannon bullet taken red hot out of the fire,
except that it was more pale and faint' and then more brightly when
the bottle was shaken.

Kraft also allowed the fellows to hold a lump of phosphorus in
their hands. With a showman's flair for the theatrical he then
shattered it into fragments all over the floor. Boyle looked on in
horror. He thought it might have burned the Turkish rug and quickly
had candles brought in, but an inspection reassured him. Out went
the candles again. Kraft's pièce de résistance was to dip his finger in
liquid phosphorus and write the word 'DOMINI' on a sheet of
paper. Boyle was entranced. He said the glowing letters seemed a
'mixture of strangeness, beauty and frightfulness'.

Boyle was a man of fittingly luminous intelligence, a bridge
between alchemy and modern chemistry. Desperate to understand
how this substance was produced and to learn its properties, he
tried to persuade Kraft to divulge where it had come from. All Kraft

would give him was the clue that phosphorus was made from something that 'belonged to the body of man'. So Boyle boiled down large volumes of urine into a paste to see what would happen.

Nothing, in fact. No unearthly glowing. No green fingers. It was only in 1679 that Boyle's assistant thought of seeking information from Hennig Brandt in Germany, the man who had first discovered phosphorus from experiments on his own urine[*]. Brandt revealed that phosphorus would only be given off if the urine residue was heated to extremely high temperatures. After trying that, Boyle was finally successful.

His method, as befits the man who first defined a chemical element as a substance that cannot be broken down,[18] was to treat the extraction as a chemical problem rather than an alchemical recipe. While Brandt had only managed to extract about 1 per cent of the phosphorus in urine, Boyle got nearly all of it. He was then able to stun his friends with the same parlour tricks that Kraft had played on him.

In 1680 Robert Boyle had another success. He coated a small piece of paper with his white phosphorus and a splinter of wood with sulphur. When he drew the sulphur-tinted wood across the paper it burst into flame. It was, in effect, the world's first matchstick.

But Icy Noctiluca proved dangerously combustible for matchsticks and it wasn't until the nineteenth century that safe commercial ones were synthetically produced with red phosphorus. For that glacially beautiful name alone, though, Boyle deserves our thanks.

Indian Yellow

IN THE MOVIE *Girl with a Pearl Earring*, based on Tracy Chevalier's novel about the making of a Vermeer masterpiece, the artist's patron embarrasses the subject of the portrait by telling her she's been glazed with cow piss. He might have said the same about the vibrant blouse of Vermeer's jug-pouring Milkmaid or any number of seventeenth-century Dutch paintings that owed their warm,

---

See: Alchemist's Reward[*]

light-fast yellows to an extraordinary pigment made from the urine of mango-eating cows.

Thanks to the efforts of an energetic Indian researcher in 1893, it is now possible to stand in a London basement with a rare specimen of Indian Yellow between your fingers and know that Vermeer's patron in the film was spot-on – although whether he could have made the jibe so accurately at the time is debateable, because for hundreds of years nobody had a clue about the true origin of this pigment.

It arrived at the shops of colourmen in cities like Antwerp, London, Paris and Vienna, smelling revolting, in the form of dusty brown balls with chunks of vivid yellow inside that were then washed and purified to make paint. Was it snake pee? Might it be urine from an animal fed on bile-coloured turmeric. Or was it obtained, as the George Rowney and Co. catalogue was still claiming as late as 1896, from 'the excrement of camels'? For centuries speculation abounded.

In 1883 the German chemist Carl Graebe was so keen to solve the mystery that he approached the Royal Gardens at Kew in London to see if its director, the great botanist and plant collector, Sir Joseph Hooker, could help. Hooker initiated inquiries with the Indian Office, which were then passed to the government of India itself. It promptly despatched a talented civil servant, Trailokya Nath Mukharji, to track down Indian Yellow.

T.N. Mukharji was a respected exhibition organiser for the British Raj, a sympathetic intermediary between the worlds of empire and colony who doggedly set out to find the truth. On 27 August 1883 he produced a report revealing what he had discovered.[19] Sources in Calcutta had told him, he wrote, that the substance known as *piuri* was made at the town of Monghyr (now Munger in Bihar). So he had set off to see for himself. In the suburbs of Monghyr, at a place called Mirzapur, he had found a sect of *gwalas*, or milkmen, who were said to be the only people who manufactured *piuri*. He watched carefully how they did it.

'They feed the cows solely with mango leaves and water, which increases the bile pigment and imparts to the urine a bright yellow colour,' he wrote, adding – with a more fastidious attention to detail than his readers may have thanked him for – that 'the cows treated with mango leaves are made to pass urine three or four times a day by having the urinary organ slightly rubbed with the hand, and they are so habituated to this process that they have become incapable of passing water of their own accord.'

He watched the urine being collected throughout the day in small earthen pots and put over a fire in the evening. 'The heat causes the yellow principle to precipitate, separating it from the watery portion,' he wrote. 'It is then strained with a small piece of cloth; the sediment is made into a ball, and dried first on charcoal fire and then in the sun, when it is ready for the market.'

Mukharji sent Sir Joseph some of the *piuri* balls, along with an earthen pot, a bottle of the special cow urine and a bunch of mango leaves. Professor Graebe in Geneva was then able to get to work on the chemistry. He deduced that 'mango leaves contain either euxanthone or a body capable of transformation in the organs of the cow into euxanthone, and this by combining with glycuronic acid produces the colouring matter. The magnesium which is an essential ingredient in Indian Yellow either comes from the food of the animal or from water.'[20]

So Indian Yellow's provenance and its chemical secrets were revealed at last and T.N. Mukharji was a hero. Recently the English writer Victoria Finlay reported her surprise at finding no folk-memory of the production of *piuri* in Mirzapur, although she did find plenty of cows and a cool garden of mango trees. She wondered if Mukharji might have made the story up.[21]

To judge for yourself you must seek out L. Cornelissen and Son in London, one of the few places in the world where you can still handle Indian Yellow. At ground level this long-established artists' supplier in Great Russell Street is a cornucopia of specialist modern art materials, but descend by special permission into the basement and you are suddenly back in history, squeezing into an Aladdin's cave of piled-high-tomes, ancient bottles and unusual paint brushes, a place where balls of pigment made from old cow-pee don't seem at all out of place.

The owner Nicholas Walt, wispily tall and bespectacled, climbs on to a green leather chair and reaches up to the top shelf, teetering down again with three glass jars, each marked 'Genuine Indian Yellow' in faded lettering. From a more modern box, incongruously branded 'The British Council: Broadcasting in Britain' ('Well, I had to find an airtight container,' sighs Mr Walt. 'You'll see why'), he then pulls a polythene bag full of what look like dusty-brown potatoes.

'The jars contain the Indian Yellow after it has been broken open. The pieces in the bag here are the way it looked when it first arrived,' he says, gliding away to weigh the bag. The small, brilliant, orangey-yellow lumps of pigment remain firmly incarcerated in their stoppered jars on the table. How many cows peed themselves into an early grave to make all of this, you wonder.

'We have about one and a half kilos in here,' Mr Walt announces, returning with the bag.

'Why don't you plunge in?' he says, proffering a kilo and a half of what is probably among the last remnants of genuine Indian Yellow in any quantity anywhere in the world. 'See what *you* think Indian Yellow is made of.'

The misshapen balls are light and powdery. They feel nothing like potatoes. And the stench rocks you back on your heels. Satisfyingly. Convincingly. There is no doubt that the unmistakeable tang of century-old urine is also indefinably but compellingly bovine. Quite enough to persuade you that Mukharji was right and Vermeer's *Girl with a Pearl Earring* did indeed have a significant brush with cow piss.

Indigo

'I'M DYEING, I'M dyeing, I'm dyeing,' William Morris once bawled theatrically to a friend who called in to visit. The brilliant nineteenth-century artist, writer and designer of wallpaper and textiles was a keen dyer whose hands, like those of his medieval counterparts, were often stained a violent blue*. The culprit was

---

See: Blue Monday*

indigo, with which Morris was experimenting for his textiles. Working with the dye-vat had made his hands a 'woeful spectacle', he reported in 1877. They probably smelled pretty bad, too.

It was the Portuguese explorer Vasco da Gama who first brought indigo from India to Europe in 1498, where it gradually overtook native woad (an inferior source of the pigment indigotin) as the blue of dyers' choice[*]. For centuries fermenting urine provided the mild alkalinity that released the dye. European dyers would often immerse the indigo in a giant vat of up to two thousand gallons of stale urine at a time, which could last for years. Woad, madder, bran, lime and ashes might also be added.

William Morris went to enormous trouble to apply the ancient techniques to his own dyes. He immersed himself in antiquarian books, mainly French tomes from the sixteenth and seventeenth centuries but even going as far back as the Roman polymath Pliny, whose recipes (which included making a ruby dye from wine mixed with the urine of an uncorrupted youth) he found 'amusing'[**]. There is no intelligence on whether Morris sought donations from boys himself, but traditional methods of dyeing indigo would certainly have necessitated the use of somebody's urine.

The urine vat held sway until ammonia became available from coal tar distillation early in the nineteenth century. William Morris, always comfortable with the traditions of bygone times, was proud to nurse an already dying art.

_____

See: **Woaδ**[*]
　　　Pliny[**]

Jellyfish

'I THINK YOU'RE great,' Monica tells Chandler at the end of one of the most fondly remembered early episodes of the American sitcom *Friends*. She smiles. Chandler's heart pounds. 'But you will always be the guy who peed on me.'

The episode was having fun with the widespread belief that urinating on jellyfish stings eases the pain. It's the one thing we all know about urine, isn't it? Pee on a sting, as the lovelorn Chandler does at the beach when Monica falls victim, and it will feel better. But will it really? Debate has raged and the jury is still out.

Jellyfish leave tiny, coiled stingers in our flesh, called nematocysts, which inject venom. The problem about working out the best way to deal with these, should you find yourself in Monica's position, is that there are lots of different kinds of jellyfish, many competing treatments, little scientific data and dozens of bickering experts.

Use hot water, says one. Hot water? The last thing you should use for jellyfish, retorts another. Fresh water will just trigger the nematocysts to inject more venom. Best to neutralise the venom with vinegar, which is acidic.

But urine is acidic, too, protests the pee school. Yes, but not always acidic enough, say others; sometimes it's alkaline. And anyway, it's 95% fresh water, so it will just fire the nematocysts.

By the way, interjects another, have you thought of scraping the site of the sting with a credit card. A credit card – are you mad? cries a medical toxicologist. Scraping it with anything will make the sting hurt more.

This toxicologist definitely sounds the most composed of the babble of jellyfish voices. He says acidic solutions like urine or vinegar *can* help with some jellyfish stings, but they will only worsen the sting from others. To be on the safe side, he concludes, just use a normal salt-water solution for any of them. Not too difficult on a beach, one would have thought.

When the jury returns, it looks as if we should expect a majority verdict against urine. But there are bound to be a few obstinate souls who refuse to concede the point because, whatever the experts say, it worked for them.

Jordan

CURVY, ROUND-BOTTOMED and full of pish, this jordan went down in the world fast. It started out as a respectable glass bottle, degenerated into a chamber-pot and ended up as a term of abuse for a silly person.

In its finest hour, a jordan (origin unknown but possibly related to the biblical river) was the bulbous flask in which medieval physicians collected urine for inspection and diagnosis. Those were the days when urine held the key to the universe[*]. Layers within it were thought to correspond to the body's four elements of fire, earth, water and air, which themselves related to the four humours holding the body in balance: earth in the black bile, fire in the yellow bile, water in the phlegm and all four elements in the blood.

The jordan put the theory into action. It was even designed to look like a bladder, with an impractically rounded bottom which prevented it standing on its own and meant it had to be propped

---

See: Uroscopy[*]

in a small wicker basket. For medieval doctors the bladder shape meant the urine could arrange itself exactly the way it was believed to be in the body itself.

The physician first judged the thickness of the urine by holding the jordan up to the light. If he could see the joints of his fingers through it, the urine was thin. Colour came next, checked against twenty standard shades ranging from watery clear to yellow, red, purple, dark green and a deeply alarming black[*]. A shake of the flask would then show up any foam or flakes. Finally, he would taste it three times for sweetness: first while fresh and warm, then after it had cooled for an hour or two, and lastly when completely cold.

The information he gleaned was supplemented by an enlightened interrogation about life-style and eating habits, of a kind that modern GPs struggle to fit into their ten-minute consultation. The final diagnosis also took account of astrological signs and the weather.

The image of a physician holding up his jordan to the light for inspection was so symbolic of the doctor's craft that by the late fourteenth century it had become a public emblem throughout Europe, the trademark of practising physicians. Even religious figures like Cosmas and Damian, patron saints of medicine, were portrayed piously inspecting one.

Later artists used the jordan as the theatrical focus of deathbed scenes so often it became a cliché. Paintings of doctors peering at urine flasks remained popular throughout Europe well into the nineteenth century.

By that time, though, the word 'jordan' was on the way out. It belonged, like the old medicine and its outdated theories, to another age. It lived on for a while as a term for a chamber-pot and in the sixteenth century provided writers like the Scots poet William Dunbar with a handy term of abuse: 'ane full plum Jurdane'. Or, as we might say, a right Jordan.

See: 𝔶ellow[*]

Judaism

THE JEWISH RELIGION, always keen on rules, dips its toe into matters urinary in the laws and ordinances known as the Halakhot. A dizzying list of what you can and cannot read in the presence of human or animal urine, at what precise distance it becomes permissible and how far you should retreat if the smell should happen to reach your nostrils, leaves you with the firm impression that it really is better to do your reading somewhere else.

Jug City

IF THE PROSPERITY of your town is built on urine, why not admit it? In fact, why not celebrate it? To this day the Dutch city of Tilburg calls itself *Kruikenstad*, or Jug City, to commemorate its glory-days as the wool capital of the Netherlands, when mill labourers were paid extra to bring their urine to work in a jug.

Its citizens are also proud to refer to themselves as *Kruikenzeikers* (people who pee in jugs or pitchers). Where other towns have statues of war heroes or worthy benefactors, Tilburg boasts a man clutching a stoppered jug. It's an acknowledgement that, as in other wool-producing areas across Europe[*], urine was once the secret of its manufacturing success.

Jumping Hamsters

IT'S NOT CLEAR what hamsters have done to deserve being singled out for humiliation in public urinals, but it seems a shame that even an electronic one has to spend its life being urinated at.

The game, designed to spice up peeing in restaurants, was invented by designers in Massachusetts and is activated by the impact of a stream of urine. Sensor wires, running from the basin to a circuit board and computer behind the toilet wall, control a group of frenetic hamsters on a screen above the urinal. Instead of whiling away the time in boring calm, possibly taking in an eye-level advert for car insurance, our man gazes at the screen and

See: Handy Pandy[*]

aims at points on the urinal that correspond to individual jumping hamsters.

'A successful hit turns a hamster yellow, makes it scream and spin out of control, and rewards the player with ten points,' explain creators Dan Maynes-Aminzade and Hayes Solos Raffle with a little too much relish.

They believe their system, 'You're in Control', will reduce spillage by motivating a decent aim and boost the sale of drinks by making getting rid of them afterwards so much more fun. They have even created a bizarre game controller for women, consisting of a nylon belt, acrylic pelvic plate, water bottles, tubing and the nozzle of a garden hose, so that everyone can share the joy of making hamsters scream.

Kangaroos

IT'S CONSIDERED BAD form to cull your national emblem. So Australians get upset when farmers and conservationists, pointing out that their favourite marsupial is a plant-damaging pest, try to have them shot or poisoned. Still, the fact remains that kangaroos who chomp happily on grazing land set aside for sheep and cattle are a serious nuisance. Now scientists are thrilled to have discovered a humane answer: the urine of the wild dog known as the dingo.

Dingos are terrifying predators to kangaroos, which can be sent into a frenzy even at the bark of a domestic dog. Trials co-ordinated by a behavioural ecologist at Curtin University in Perth have revealed that carefully placed dingo urine will make them head for the hills at the first sniff.

However, isolating urine from these wild dogs, keeping it fresh and shipping it across the country packed with liquid nitrogen is a complicated and expensive business, so scientists are now trying to produce a synthetic version to keep farmers happy and the iconic kangaroos in their place.

𝔎isses!

'THIS IS ONE target men will never miss,' cooed Virgin Atlantic, as it unveiled plans to install two urinals in the shape of a pair of puckered red lips in a new clubhouse at New York's JFK Airport. Unfortunately for the airline, protesting women targeted it instead.

The company professed itself astonished by the torrent of complaints the conveniences unleashed. Hang on a minute, its spokesman squeaked in defence, this urinal was even designed by a woman. Indeed in the Netherlands, where Meike van Schijndel had come up with the design for a Dutch bathroom company, 'Kisses!' (with exclamation mark) was considered amusingly ironic. Not so in America, where the president of the National Organisation of Women was tight-lipped with outrage. 'I don't know many men who think it's cool to pee in a woman's mouth, even a porcelain one,' declared Kim Gandy primly.

Virgin Atlantic knew when it was beaten and decided not to install the Kisses! urinals after all. A McDonald's restaurant in the Netherlands removed another one after an American patron complained to the U.S. head office. But the Dutch company selling them, Bathroom Mania, revelled in the publicity. They put out a straight-faced statement protesting that Kisses! was 'a sexless, cartoonish sculpture of a mouth' which was never intended to cause offence.

Leather

SUMERIAN CHARIOT DECORATIONS, Roman armour, Saxon shoes and gorgeous medieval book-bindings can all trace their origins to a vat of urine. As long as humans have hunted animals and known the benefits of leather, they have reached for this handiest of detergents to remove hair from animal hides, dissolve grease and keep the skin pliable.

Tanning – the process of preserving skins from decomposition – was in every way a smelly business, historically relegated to the outskirts of towns next to the people too poor to escape the stench. The tanneries reeked not only of stale urine, collected in so-called 'piss-pots' left on street corners, but of animal faeces and decaying flesh as well, which people were employed to collect. There is a folk memory in Newcastle-upon-Tyne of collectors known as 'dog-shit men' whose job was to gather up as much as they could find for the tanners.

The dog dung was kneaded into the skin to make it supple, with pigeon droppings also used for the purpose. The hides were sometimes soaked in a solution of animal brains, prompting one wit to coin the saying that every animal possesses just enough brains to preserve its own hide – alive or dead.

However unpleasant to live with, the old methods of tanning lasted for centuries and are still pongily prevalent in parts of the world today. In the Moroccan bazaars of Marrakesh, for instance, European tourists purchase pretty bedroom slippers in soft dyed leather, blissfully unaware that they have been prepared with camel pee.

Even after leather has been tanned in modern synthetic chemicals, it will still respond to a splash of urine. Soldiers on long marches during both world wars used to swear by peeing on their stiff regulation boots to soften the leather and prevent their feet rubbing painfully as they walked. Equestrians have been known to advocate it for new riding boots and American cowboys claim there is nothing better for making their own macho footwear a little more pliable.

In cold countries urinating in your shoe used to have the added benefit of warming up your feet. The drawback was that the effect didn't last. The Icelandic saying, *að pissa í skóinn sinn* (literally, to pee in one's shoe), lives on as a metaphor for solving a problem in a way that will exacerbate it in the long run. Your feet just end up colder.

Lichen

IT IS DIFFICULT to imagine how two such rank pongs as sheep fleece and stale urine can combine to produce a fragrance that sends woollen workers into rhapsodies. 'It was a lovely smell, really lovely. You couldn't get it anywhere else,' says Ina Morrison, dreamily recalling the scent of Harris Tweed. 'The urine was smelly and the wool of the sheep smelled too, but together they changed into something else'*.

In the French dye centres of Limoges, Clermand-Ferrand and Lyon, dyers specialising in a gorgeous hue called lichen purple would have understood what she meant. This was a dye that took weeks to perfect, so labour-intensive that it secured employment in France until the middle of the nineteenth century. Urine was the source of the nitrogen that released the rich purple from the plant

See: Harris Tweed*

and it could take a month of stirring and fermenting to hone the colour to perfection.

At the end of the process, after dyers who had been breathing in ammonia fumes for weeks wiped their streaming eyes, they were rewarded with what must have seemed a gift from heaven. The mysterious urinary alchemy had turned base pee into golden fragrance. '*Une agréable odeur de violette,*' was how a M. Cocq described it in a memoire in 1812.[22] We should probably take him at his word, for who knows his scents better than a Frenchman?

£ife of 𝔓i

IT WILL NOT have escaped readers of the 2002 Man Booker prize-winner that *Life of Pi* was within a big-cat's whisker of being *Life of Pee*.

The young Indian protagonist of Yann Martel's best-selling novel starts life as Piscine Patel (after a French swimming pool, naturally), but finds his name relentlessly mispronounced as 'Pissing' Patel.

'The words would waft across the yard to my ears, unprovoked, uncalled for: "Where's Pissing? I've got to go." Or: "You're facing the wall. Are you Pissing?"'

Made miserable by a life of pee, the boy contracts his name to Pi. The new identity proves useful in a number of ways. First, it deflects attention from pee, which is a considerable relief to the lad. Second, by the time Pi is cast adrift in a lifeboat with a 450-pound Bengal tiger, the mind-bending nature of π – a number that can never be pinned down – has already revved up our imaginations for the fantastical voyage into belief and story on which *Life of Pi* invites us.

Most importantly, the name-change frees up the alternative title for more down-to-earth publications.

Lindisfarne Gospels

IT'S GORGEOUS — ONE of the most ravishing works of religious art anywhere. Created in a monastery on England's north-east coast in the early eighth century, the *Lindisfarne Gospels* owe their opulent illustrations to one single artist-scribe. He gathered many of the raw materials on his own wind-battered island and used urine, the most local ingredient of all, to prepare several for action on the page.

The scribe, thought to be a monk called Eadfrith who became Bishop of Lindisfarne in 698 and died in 721, assembled his palette of colours with the flair of a chemist. Some of the forty or more pigments were made from exotic imports like *lapis lazuli*, a piercing blue rock from the Himalayas, ground into powder for paint. But it was to plants on his own doorstep such as woad, lichens and turnsole that Eadfrith turned for many of the purples, crimsons and more domestic shades of blue that he used to enliven the Latin text.

Crucially, it was soaking these plants in urine that released the colours[*]. Home produced Lindisfarne pee also did its bit for the green shades that owed their lustre to verdigris, made with urine and egg-whites[**][23].

The 259 pages of vellum on which Eadfrith plied his goose-feather pens and his stunningly early version of a lead pencil were made from 130 calfskins. The Lindisfarne monks are thought to have soaked these in lime and water before stretching, scraping and drying them. But in the preparation of some of Europe's other precious calfskin manuscripts it was urine, rather than lime, that loosened the flesh and hair of the skinned beasts[***].

Among the priceless literary gems that owe their vellum to urine is Ireland's national treasure, the *Book of Kells*, another gorgeously illuminated gospel manuscript from around 800, and Iceland's *Flatey Book*, largest of the revered manuscripts preserving that country's medieval sagas.

See: **Woad**[*]
Verdigris[**]
Leather[***]

Lister

THE FATHER OF antisepsis was walking home through a Glasgow park when he heard about an exhilarating discovery in Paris. Joseph Lister, who had become professor of surgery in the city in 1859 at the age of only thirty-three, listened avidly as a university colleague described how the French chemist Louis Pasteur had established that putrefaction was caused by micro-organisms in the air which caused matter to ferment.

Lister immediately spotted the relevance to his own medical research. In Glasgow Royal Infirmary, as many as half of his amputation cases had died between 1861 and 1865 from wound sepsis. He was urgently seeking a solution.

Taking note of how Pasteur had boiled a liquid broth and exposed it to the air in specially shaped flasks, Lister now tried the same experiment on his own urine. Like Pasteur, he used flasks with a bent swan-like tube attached and found that, while urine in normal straight-necked flasks decomposed when exposed to the air, the twisted neck seemed to trap the microbes. Air was passing through but the urine remained uncontaminated.

From this, Lister concluded that the answer to the appallingly high levels of post-surgery deaths from infected wounds was to exclude germs in the air. He began experimenting by covering surgical wounds with lint covered in creosote and, later, carbolic acid. While Queen Victoria was at Balmoral he even, rather daringly, sterilised a piece of rubber tubing this way and used it as a drain for an abcess in the royal armpit. In 1867 he reported that his wards in Glasgow Royal Infirmary had remained clear of sepsis for nine months.

It took a long time for Lister to convince a patronising medical establishment of the theory he had developed from observing urine. But his methods eventually brought an overwhelming reduction in the incidence of wound infection.

Lister was keen on urinary experiments. When he moved to the other side of Scotland to become professor of surgery at Edinburgh's renowned medical school, he became the first person to grow bacteria in pure culture. One experiment involved putting urine into a sterile glass and allowing some Edinburgh rain to fall on it: he was able to see both bacteria and yeasts in the resultant cultures.

In 1871, nearly 60 years before Alexander Fleming spotted the antibiotic properties of penicillin by the chance contamination of a bacterial culture, Lister was already describing how urine samples contaminated with mould prohibited the growth of bacteria; he also described the antibacterial action on human tissue of what he called *Penicillium Glaucum**.

According to one authority, Lister kept some of the very urine used in his original swan-necked experiment for many years. It appeared as sterile 'as if it had just been drawn'.[24]

Luther

THE CATHOLIC MONK turned Protestant reformer, Martin Luther, had a flair for both the theatrical and the vulgar, so the report that he almost drowned in his own urine in 1537 is entirely fitting.

In October 1517 Luther instigated the Protestant Reformation by nailing 95 theses to a church door in Wittenberg, arguing against papal abuse and the sale of divine forgiveness. Nearly twenty years later, with Christendom already turned upside down by his theology of salvation by grace, this brash, brilliant, intemperate, larger-than-life character was at a political meeting in Schmalkalden, in Hesse, in desperate pain from kidney stones.

He later described how his doctors had tried everything they could think of to shift the stones, which form when salts and minerals from urine crystallise, often causing a blockage which makes it difficult – and in his case impossible – to urinate. 'I was so terribly tormented by the doctors,' he wrote. 'They gave me as much to drink as if I were a huge ox and treated all my limbs, even sucking at my private parts.'

None of this faintly astonishing treatment worked. Luther's

See: 𝔓enicillin*

physician, Matthäus Ratzberger, reported that his patient's whole body had become so bloated that 'one could do nothing for him but expect the end'. So Luther asked if he could be taken home to Saxony to die.

Fatally ill, he rattled homewards in a carriage to meet his Maker. But on the rough roads from Hesse to Saxony he was so bumped about that something within him shifted. In the early hours of 27 February 1537, reported his physician, the stone was dislodged and Luther 'almost drowned in his own water'.

Herr Dr Ratzberger, who clearly had a flair for overstatement himself, added that Luther never recovered from his kidney stones. The theologian also suffered monumental bouts of constipation, which necessitated such lengthy sessions on the toilet that he managed to work out his entire reformed theology while stuck there. German archaeologists reckon they have found the very lavatory from which he launched the Reformation in the garden of his house in Wittenberg.

Luther lived for another nine years after the life-saving urination, but they were not his finest. He unwisely sanctioned the bigamy of Philip I, Landgrave of Hesse, which damaged his reputation, and published inflammatory works against the Jews, on which the Nazis would one day seize to justify their anti-Semitism.

After the kidney-stone drama Martin Luther wrote: 'Had I died of my stones in Schmalkalden, I would already have been in Heaven for a year now, free of all ills.' There are some who wonder if it might not have been better all round if relief had indeed not come to the great man when it did.

Manneken Pis

THE SMALL BRONZE sculpture of a chubby boy peeing into the basin of a fountain is Brussels' most famous landmark, which tells you something about the capital of Belgium. Nobody has the faintest idea why the *Manneken Pis* (Dutch for *Little Man Urinating*) is there or what the boy is supposed to commemorate, but it's safe to say his pulling power beats the offices of the European Commission, the birthplace of Tintin's creator Hergé and possibly even the city's line in praline chocolate.

One legend has the two-year-old Duke Godfrey III of Leuven being hung in a basket from a tree in the twelfth century to encourage his troops in battle and then to urinate on their foes. Another has a boy saving Brussels from a besieging foreign power by peeing on a burning fuse to prevent an explosion that would have brought down the city walls. The most sentimental story commemorates a little boy lost, who was later found by his father happily urinating in a garden. All that is known for sure is that in 1619 the city ordered the sculptor Jerome Duquesnoy to make a new bronze statue to replace an ancient one.

There the boy stands, peeing for Belgium, sometimes hooked

up to a keg of beer and frequently dressed in extremely bizarre clothes. His first outfit arrived in 1698 from the governor of the Austrian Netherlands and he now has more than 600 in his wardrobe, including Elvis Presley gear and a Mickey Mouse costume. The clothes are ceremonially changed to the accompaniment of a brass band.

Naturally, in this most politically correct of cities, there is also a *Jeanneke Pis* – a grey limestone statue of a pigtailed girl squatting amiably. Made by Denis-Adrien Debouvrie, Jeanneke began peeing into her own fountain in 1987.

To be fair, you can find statues of peeing boys all over Belgium, if not yet peeing girls. The city of Geraardsbergen, whose citizens stand accused of having once stolen the rival statue from Brussels, claims its *Mannekin Pis* is actually the oldest.

Marathon Runners

RUNNING FOR TWENTY-SIX miles against the clock involves some sharp urinary decisions for the serious marathon runner, for whom diverting into one of the hundreds of portable toilets is not an option that will win you the race.

Do you just relieve yourself wherever you happen to be – into a passing bush, say? Residents along the route of the Boston Marathon became so fed up with runners urinating in their gardens that they put up signs warning of video camera surveillance. 'On any other day of the year, they'd be arrested and put on the state sex offender lists for public lewdness,' grumbled one Boston homeowner.

And what about the start of the race? The really keen runners, who calculate exactly how much they need to drink for hydration before the race and then empty their bladders as often as they can until just before it begins, say there is nothing worse than having to stand in a toilet queue with the race about to start. So they get on with it there and then. At the New York Marathon punch-ups were reported between athletes who accidentally peed on each other at the start-line.

Even when you have worked out your hydration to the last sip and the final pre-race pee, chances are you may still have to urinate during the race as you top up with fluids. In that case the elite runners advise overcoming a lifetime of social training and letting go as you run. Men and women alike find this a messy option but resort to it all the same.

And if you really don't care who is looking, you can always try world record-holder Paula Radcliffe's technique during the 2005 London Marathon, when she halted fleetingly at the 22-mile mark to squat by the side of the road in full view of astonished onlookers and the world's media. This was less of a pee-stop than the reaction of her stomach to her pre-race meal, another hazard for the long-distance runner. 'I was losing time because I was having stomach cramps and I thought 'I just need to go and I'll be fine,' Radcliffe explained afterwards. Her winning time of two hours and seventeen minutes was the third fastest ever, so who are we to argue?

Marilyn Monroe

THE FILMMAKER BILLY Wilder gave Marilyn Monroe all her best acting roles and himself all the best lines. A man of whom friends observed that beneath his gruff exterior was a gruff interior, he described her as having 'breasts of granite and a mind like a Gruyère cheese'. He also told a story about Monroe spending a penny at her mother-in-law's house which might even be true.

By the time she worked with Wilder on the fifties comedy *Some Like It Hot*, the former model was married to the playwright Arthur Miller. Wilder recounted that after the couple became engaged, Miller had taken Monroe to meet his mother, who lived in a miniscule flat with paper-thin walls in New York.

'So they go there,' Wilder recalled, 'to that tiny little apartment, with a kind of very flimsy door between the living room and the toilet. They're having a very good time, they get along great, and then Marilyn Monroe says she's got to go the WC, the toilet. And she goes, and because the walls are thin, she turns on all the faucets so they would not hear it in the next room. Now she comes out, and everything's beautiful, kiss, kiss.

'Next day, Arthur calls the mother and says, "How did you like her?" And the mother says, "She's sweet, a wonderful, wonderful, wonderful girl. But she pisses like a horse."'

Mortars

BATTLE IS RAGING. Your mortars are working overtime but they start to overheat and the Allied advance depends on those bombs continuing to fly over the hill. What do you do? If you're Captain Jock Bannister of the 1st Worcestershires, you reach for the nearest coolant to hand and order the rest of the platoon to do the same. You then go down in regimental history as the man who instigated a mass urination that helped to save the push on Tilly.

Bannister led the regiment's mortar platoon. On 27 August 1944 his mortars were pumping ammunition from their short, wide-bored tubes over the top of the hill. 'They had been firing continuously,' he recalled, 'and they had all overheated. As soon as a mortar bomb was put into the barrel, its primary charge was igniting and the bombs were falling only twenty yards away.'

Somehow or other those mortars had to be cooled down. The captain had an idea. His duty was clear. 'I lined up my men,' he reported chirpily, 'and got them to pee on the barrels by numbers.'

There were precedents for Bannister's quick thinking. The machine guns which dominated the battlefields of the Great War had also suffered from excessive heat. In fact, the early ones were so primitive that they sometimes overheated within two minutes. Wrapping them in water-filled jackets cooled the guns down well enough, but this meant having large supplies of water on hand to replenish the jackets. If the water ran out, machine gun crews resorted to the tactic which was to prove so successful for the 1st Worcestershires thirty years later: they urinated into the jacket.

Today soldiers in the field still find urine a useful way of cooling down the noise-reducing suppressor on a rifle. Those who admit trying it as a suppressor coolant say that in the middle of a firefight there is nothing to beat urine for convenience and effectiveness. A quick pee is also said to work wonders as a lubricant if you get sand in your weapon.

Mozart

IN THE AUTUMN of 1787 Wolfgang Amadeus Mozart travelled by coach to Prague for the premiere of his opera *Don Giovanni*. At Raschala the pigtailed composer called on the coachman to stop and hopped out to relieve himself. Then he continued on his way, leaving locals gazing in wonderment at the mark of the maestro. 'We must remember this exact spot,' they told each other excitedly.

Well, it's an unlikely scenario. But that hasn't stopped the modern residents of Raschala erecting an impressive slab of granite to commemorate the spot where Mozart reputedly left his mark. Since it went up in 1976, the *Pinkelstein*, or pee-stone, has generated more interest in Mozart's piddle in this pocket of lower Austria than in his music.

Hordes of tourists head there to read the solemn inscription: 'In the year 1787 Wolfgang Amadeus Mozart on his journey to Prague got his coach to stop at precisely this spot. Since then this stone has been popularly known as the Pee-Stone.'[25] Another notice requests that visitors refrain from the regrettable urge to do some pinkling there themselves. The stone is a wildly successful marketing ploy, and nobody seems remotely bothered by the question of whether the famous pee-stop ever actually happened.

We do know it was Mozart's second trip that year to the former Bohemian capital. The previous January his opera *Le Nozze di Figaro* had proved such a roaring success in Prague that another was commissioned, one he would complete in the nick of time and conduct to a rapturous reception on 29 October. The sublime arias of *Don Giovanni* must already have been soaring in his head as he set off that September on the 252-mile journey from his home in Vienna.

His coach would indeed have taken the main road running north-west from Vienna to Prague, which ran through the tiny community of Raschala. But the coach would then have halted just a mile further on in the town of Hollabrun, where there was a post-station and rest for the horses. Why then, an assiduous pee-detective might inquire, would a traveller not hold on for just a few minutes longer to spend a penny in comfort there?

The 340 inhabitants of modern Raschala have no time for such historical introspection. They jumped at the suggestion when one of their residents, an architecture professor, suggested exploiting the old saying that this place was so boring that even Mozart only stopped there long enough to take a leak. Rumour has it that the professor actually invented the coach-stop himself during a tipsy night out with friends in 1975, the year before the stone went up. It matters not, for the *Pinkelstein* has revolutionised Raschala's fortunes and they love it.

Mozart, who once said he wrote music as a sow piddles, would doubtless find it all hugely amusing.

Mud Bricks

VICTORIA HARRIS DIDN'T exactly shout 'Eureka!' There were fifty people in the conference room and she didn't want to make a scene. But she did scrawl 'URINE' in capital letters across her notepad and shoved it towards a colleague, who raised a thoughtful eyebrow. The English physicist had suddenly thought of a solution to the monstrous reconstruction problems in war-blighted Darfur.

Dr Harris, then chief executive of the UK charity Article 25 (which at the time was called Architects for Aid) was in Geneva. She was listening to a dispirited UN-Habitat official explaining that it would take more timber than the total number of trees in the whole of Sudan to build wooden shelters for all of Darfur's displaced multitudes. No water could be spared for making mud-bricks, either, because every drop was needed for drinking.

Suddenly, Dr Harris had the answer. 'The idea just popped into my head,' she says. 'If the water's needed for drinking, why can't we mix the bricks from water *after* it's been drunk?'

Back home she asked Jeremy Till, director of architecture at Sheffield University, to find out whether urine could indeed replace water in the construction of mud-bricks. Not a man to shy from an unorthodox building challenge (his own house is constructed of straw-bales), Professor Till set a team of students to work. With urine collected from bemused friends they made several hundred bricks.

The experiments were thorough and the bricks were dried, pummelled, crushed and sniffed. They were pounded with water jets as fierce as any storm. After ten weeks the team concluded that, thanks to the qualities of urea as a binding agent, the bricks were actually tougher and more resilient than those made with fresh water. Constructing a basic mud-brick shelter with urine was practicable, safe and would take a family of four about two years to complete.[26]

Article 25 is now urging collaborators to start building with urine in those parts of the world in direst need of emergency housing. All people would need is urine-diverting toilets, already common in refugee camps, and storage. According to Victoria Harris, the natural breakdown of urea into ammonia, plus the effects of sunlight, would destroy any bacteria and viruses.

With nearly 24 million people internally displaced in about 50 countries and water there in desperately short supply, her message is that with will and imagination wee can fix it.

Muhammad

THE PROPHET MUHAMMAD advocated a tot of camel's urine as a medicine and Bedouin tribesmen still swear by its potency. Arab scientists have lately been putting this Sunni Muslim belief to the test in the laboratory, confirming a long list of health benefits which include the easing of digestive problems, curing of dropsy and healing of wounds. As an experiment Professor Ahmad 'Abd-Allaah Ahmadaani, dean of the Faculty of Medical Sciences in the Sudanese al-Jazeerah University, gave patients suffering cirrhosis of the liver (from the deadly tropical disease bilharzia) a daily dose of camel's urine, and reportedly found they all responded well.

Across the Arab world this ancient Islamic remedy is becoming fashionable again. According to the Arab TV network al-Arabiya, hair salons in the Yemen are buying camel urine and selling it on with the claim that it strengthens the scalp, slows balding and promotes healthy hair. Business is good these days for camel breeders.

Neigh Oestrogen

EVERY WINTER HUNDREDS of prairie horse farmers in the Canadian provinces of Manitoba, Saskatchewan and Alberta, and the American state of North Dakota collect a load of urine from 60,000 pregnant mares and ship it to the Canadian city of Brandon. There oestrogen is extracted and sent on to New York and Montreal to be turned into Premarin, an HRT drug commonly used to treat symptoms of menopause all over the world.

Women unaware of the provenance of the creams and tablets prescribed for their hot flushes may have missed the clue in the name, blithely coined from PREgnant MAREs' urINe. Just as the hormones in nuns' urine helped doctors to pioneer infertility treatment for younger women[*], so the oestrogen in horse pee is a cornerstone of hormone replacement therapy for the middle-aged. Replacing the slight fall in natural oestrogen levels during the menopause has made Premarin a top-selling product for Wyeth-Ayerst, the multinational pharmaceutical company now merged with the giant Pfizer.

See: Nuns[*]

Taking urine from pregnant mares is controversial, however. There are strict government and company guidelines for horse welfare, but animal rights campaigners complain loudly about conditions in the Canadian 'pee farms', as they call them. The lobby group HorseAid claims that mares, producing ninety to a hundred gallons of urine throughout the collection season from October to March, are kept on a pregnancy conveyor belt and confined for the last six months in cramped stalls. They also say too many foals are sent to slaughter.

Horse Aid's slogan: 'Just Say Neigh to Premarin.'

New Zealand Wine

A GROUP OF wine experts spent six years and $12 million trying to define the flavour of New Zealand's renowned *sauvignon blanc*. The wine-quaffing world waited breathlessly and in 2009 they announced their conclusion. The flavour of *sauvignon blanc*, let it be revealed, is sweaty passion-fruit, asparagus and cat urine.

Now, there are two ways for wine-makers to react to a judgement like that. They can shuffle their feet and hope nobody was listening. Or they can tell everyone brightly that the flavour of cat pee makes wine 'complex' and 'interesting', which is how New Zealanders reacted to the news. One of the country's wineries even dubbed its white wine 'Cat's Pee on a Gooseberry Bush'.

Nuns

THE URINE OF post-menopausal Italian nuns is unlikely to leap into a woman's mind when she contemplates fertility treatment, but for a long time this was the secret ingredient in a drug that gave childless women hope. The nuns' hormones helped to conceive the world's first test-tube baby in 1978 and Britain's first test-tube twins in 1982.

What made those middle-aged nuns so valuable is that women going through the menopause produce large amounts of hCG (human chorionic gonadotropin), as their bodies try in vain to revive the pegged-out conception process. Harvest those hormones and you can use them to stimulate ovulation in younger women who are struggling to conceive.

For the Serono biotech company, who pioneered the fertility technology in 1949, it was a daunting business to source enough post-menopausal urine to supply the production of their drug Pergonal. The nuns from a convent near the company's headquarters in Rome were the right age, conveniently grouped together for urine collection purposes and, one assumes, happy to donate to the promotion of human life. (Maybe no-one told them the Roman Catholic Church believes *in vitro* fertilisation is a mortal sin.) By the time Pergonal's popularity had reached its height, the company (later renamed Ares-Serona and headquartered in Geneva) was ferrying tanker-loads of urine across the world from donors as far away as Brazil and Argentina.

These days so-called 'recombinant' technology, using genetically modified Chinese hamster ovary cells, is increasingly popular as an alternative source of hormones. But human urine continues to play its part. Meanwhile, there must be hundreds, perhaps thousands, of women across the world who owe a joyful family life to those anonymous Italian nuns.

Obnoxious

CAN YOU SEND pee in the post if it's not for medical purposes? The question was raised by the case of a 47-year-old American from Washington who took exception to being fined for driving too fast in the neighbouring northwest state of Oregon, where speed limits are lower. He vented his feelings by emptying $206 in extremely small change into a plastic bag, soaking the whole lot in urine and sending it to the payments division of the local court in a box.

The sheriff's sergeant who opened the box in Portland was not happy. 'The pile of coins emitted a strong, pungent odour of stale urine,' he reported stiffly. 'This was very concerning to me.'

Sergeant Phil Anderchuk got straight on to the US postal service to see if any federal law had been broken. But he was told it was not against the law to mail a box of bodily fluids as long as it was properly packed and did not emit an 'obnoxious odour'. On retorting that the odour was obnoxious enough for him, the sergeant was told that being blasted with a smell AFTER you open the package doesn't count.

Sergeant Anderchuk might have had better luck with the UK's Royal Mail service. It is relaxed about obnoxious pee as long as it's securely contained, but does ban material that could be described (by two other heavy-duty *o*-words) as 'obscene' or 'offensive'. Would that include a bag of urine-soaked coins posted with the express intention of offending? We await a test-case.

Back in Oregon the sergeant gave up trying to interest the law in his plight. He sealed the box up again and sent it back empty to Mr Michael Lynch, of Bellevue, Washington, inviting him to pay $27.30 for postage if he wanted his small change back. He also demanded immediate payment of the fine – by cheque.

On Guard

WITH THE FOUNTAINS of the Victoria Memorial squirting merrily beyond the railings, a sentry's two-hour stint of duty at Buckingham Palace can challenge the strongest bladder. There stand the guardsmen in their bearskin hats and scarlet uniforms, gaping tourist eyes upon them, desperate for a pee and with nowhere to go.

In times of more bracing army discipline, succumbing to that call could land a guardsman in big trouble. Infantryman Len Waller, busy guarding the King's residence in 1940 before his battalion of Grenadier Guards was sent to the front, was appalled to discover that 'going behind the sentry box for a crafty pee when there was nobody about and forgetting that the evidence might still be there when the sergeant did his rounds' meant arrest and arduous punishment. Blaming it on a dog never worked. At worst the misdemeanour could spell time in the notorious 'glasshouse' military prison, and at the very least a wearying hour of extra drill carrying full equipment.

These days if a guardsman badly needs to be relieved, in every sense, he can be saved by the bell. Soldiers from the Scots Guards, Irish Guards, Welsh Guards, Grenadier Guards or Coldstream Guards, who stand motionless for the requisite two hours in front of their toy houses trying not to count the minutes before the next four-hour break, have recourse to a bell in the sentry box. But you only do this, warns one ex-Coldstream Guardsman severely, as a very last resort.

Oral Rinse

THE MAN THEY call the father of modern dentistry, Pierre Fauchard, introduced the reclining dentist's chair, ivory false teeth, wire braces, amalgam fillings and regular cleaning. His descriptions of oral anatomy, pathology, disease and dental operations were the first complete scientific description of dentistry. It was he who insisted it was sugar, not tiny worms, that made teeth rot. He also advocated rinsing in urine for healthy teeth and gums.

All these innovations are discussed in the two-volume, 863-page tome, *Le Chirurgien Dentiste* (The Surgeon Dentist), published in 1728. In it Fauchard advocates a method of bringing relief to patients with rotten teeth who are tormented by aches and pains. 'It consists of rinsing out the mouth every morning and also evening … with some spoonfuls of their own urine, just after it has been passed.'

Fauchard felt bound to add a caveat about the urine rinse, though 'It is true that it is not very agreeable,' he wrote, 'except inasmuch as it brings distinct relief.' You can almost hear the sigh as he adds: 'But what will one not do for relief and for health?'

Orion

ORION, THE GIANT huntsman of Greek mythology who gave his name to a mighty constellation, was conceived exactly as every pun-lover might hope: in a stream of divine urine.

According to at least one of the legends about his parentage, the gods Zeus, Poseidon and Hermes arrived one day to visit the childless Hyrieus of Boeotia, who roasted a bull in their honour. In return for his hospitality, they offered Hyrieus his heart's desire. He asked at once for a son. Nothing easier, said the gods. They promptly urinated on the bull's hide, buried it in the earth and told the bemused Hyrieus to dig it up ten months later. When he did, he found a child. It certainly beats pregnancy.

The Roman poet Ovid reports that Hyrieus called the boy *Urion* (from the Greek *ouron*, meaning urine) in deference to his mode of birth. 'Then,' he explains, 'the first letter lost its ancient sound.' Sadly Ovid's derivation is as much a fiction as the story itself.

Another stab at etymology tempted the seventh-century scholar Isidore of Seville to conclude in his twenty-volume encyclopaedia that the constellation Orion owes its name to the Latin *urina* for quite a different reason. 'It is named Orion from urine, that is, from a flood of waters. For it rises in the winter season, and troubles the sea and the land with waters and storms.'

Whatever its derivation, Orion has struggled to shed its urinary associations. It was a gift to the pun-loving astronaut Wally Schirra, who liked to boast that he had 'peed all over the world' during his 1965 spaceflight in command of Gemini 6A. Schirra was so captivated by the starry shower of golden ice crystals formed by sending a stream of pee into space[*] that he took colour photographs and ordered a set of prints on his return to earth. He took these along to a po-faced astronomy debriefing and displayed them casually on the table alongside genuine celestial snaps.

'Gentlemen,' he announced solemnly, 'this is the constellation Urion.'

Orson Welles

A MAN WHO made his name by terrifying the citizenry of the USA into shooting at a farmer's water-tower in the belief it was a Martian tripod, would have had no hesitation in tricking guests with what he claimed was a urine-indicator dye. The American actor and director Orson Welles – whose radio presentation of *The War of the Worlds* in 1938 convinced many gullible listeners that an invasion from Mars was underway – persuaded his house-guests that he had a chemical in his swimming pool which could detect the presence of pee.

Welles told his biographer Barbara Leaming that it was always 'the nicest, cleanest, most respectable people' who relieved themselves while swimming. Obsessed with keeping his pool free of this secret contamination, he claimed to have policed it with a

See: Space[*]

chemical that caused raspberry-coloured clouds to billow in the water around any guilty swimmer. Since there is no chemical yet developed which can detect urine in water[*], it was another of the practical jokes in which Orson Welles delighted.

Perhaps the obese Welles should just have got on with swimming in the pool. It was only in the last six months of his life, with his sights set on playing King Lear, that the vast actor took to doing twenty laps a day and peeled off fifty pounds. Convinced that anyone with a private pool must have extensively peed in it, he reputedly refused to swim in any but his own.

A pity there was no dye to reveal whether he treated his pool as he believed every other owner did.

_____

See: 𝔖wimming 𝔓ools[*]

Patton

IN THE FINAL push for Allied victory in 1945, U.S. General George S. Patton beat his British arch-rival, Field Marshall Montgomery, across the River Rhine by one day. Patton's Third Army crossed Germany's great river late on the night of 22 March. When Patton himself made the crossing, he paused to enact a ritual humiliation of the enemy that he had been promising his troops for months. Ordering his driver to stop on the bridge, he relieved himself enthusiastically into the Rhine.

The general is said to have been filling up on fluids all day so that he could do justice to the occasion. Later he recorded in his diary: 'I drove to the Rhine River and went across on the pontoon bridge. I stopped in the middle to take a piss and then picked up some dirt on the far side in emulation of William the Conqueror' (who is supposed to have stumbled when he landed in 1066, leapt up with his hands full of soil and shouted, 'See I already have England in my hands'). Britain's Prime Minister Winston Churchill would follow suit with his own ceremonial pee in the Rhine some days later[*].

See: Churchill[*]

Patton followed up the crossing by calling General Bradley. 'For God's sake tell the world we're across,' he said. 'I want the world to know the Third Army made it before Monty starts across.'

He then took a swipe at General Eisenhower, commander of the Supreme Headquarters Allied Expeditionary Force, who had earlier annoyed Patton by diverting supplies to Montgomery. His message to Ike was to the point: 'Dear SHAEF, I have just pissed into the Rhine River. For God's sake, send some gasoline.'

𝔓enicillin

PENICILLIN HAS WONDERFULLY transformed the course of medicine and human health, but it was so expensive and difficult to make in the beginning that it had to be recovered from the first patient's urine and given to him again. That urine very nearly saved Albert Alexander's life.

When the reserve police constable arrived at hospital in Oxford in December 1940 with an infected scratch on his cheek, pathology professor Howard Florey and biochemist Ernst Chain were working on the first medical applications of penicillin at a university laboratory nearby. The antibiotic properties of the fungus had been discovered by Alexander Fleming in 1928, but never seriously tried on anyone. When they heard there was a patient at the Radcliffe Infirmary with a staphylococcal infection advancing so lethally through his body that he would soon die, Florey and Chain believed it was time to put penicillin to the test.

On 12 February 1941 they got permission from doctors to treat PC Alexander with the small quantity of penicillin they had painstakingly extracted from hundreds of litres of fermentation liquid. With what seemed almost incredible speed, the policeman began to recover. Within just twenty-four hours of the first 200mg injection his temperature had dropped, his appetite was returning and the infection was retreating.

But it was soon clear that Florey's small stock of penicillin would not stretch far enough to wipe out such a strong bacterial invasion completely. Casting around in desperation for a means of extending the supply, the team hit on urine. Knowing that more than half a dose of penicillin would pass through Alexander's body unchanged, they resolved to re-use it.

Each morning one of the team collected the policeman's urine from the hospital by bicycle and rushed it back to the lab – an errand they dubbed the 'P-Patrol' – and there began a heroic race against time to extract the penicillin. The amounts recovered were pitifully small,[27] but the recycled penicillin did prolong the healing process for a few more days. Sadly, however, it just wasn't long enough to save the policeman. When the recycled antibiotic finally petered out, infection started to return. Albert Alexander died on 15 March 1941.

Still, the evidence that penicillin had worked was indisputable. Funding which had been impossible to come by earlier now led to large-scale Anglo-American production. Fleming's historic discovery could at last be deployed to tackle infection in a world at war. In 1945 he shared the Nobel Prize in Physiology or Medicine with Florey and Chain.

𝔓epys

WITH OLIVER CROMWELL dead, the monarchy restored and Samuel Pepys poised to record his every move, Charles II arrived at Westminster Abbey on 23 April 1661 for his coronation. Already king of Scots, the returned exile accepted the English crown amid scenes of wild rejoicing and glittering pageantry. There in the audience was London's great diarist, desperate to relieve himself.

Fortunately Pepys did manage to capture the flavour of the coronation before he had to dash out. The 28-year-old clerk to the Navy Board had been waiting on top of a great scaffold erected across the north end of the abbey from 4 a.m. till the king arrived at 11am – a feat which would test anyone's self-control – and he was lapping up the atmosphere.

He described the abbey 'raised in the middle, all covered with red, and a throne (that is a chair) and footstool on the top of it; and all the officers of all kinds, so much as the very fidlers in red vests.' He detailed the regal procession when it arrived at last, the dignitaries in their magnificent robes, and finally the bareheaded king 'with a sceptre (carried by my Lord Sandwich) and sword and mond before him, and the crown too.'

Once the king had been crowned (a moment Pepys missed because his view was blocked but which he heard marked by 'a great shout'), he reported the thrice-repeated proclamation that 'if any one could show any reason why Charles Stewart should not be King of England, that now he should come and speak. And a Generall Pardon also was read by the Lord Chancellor, and meddalls flung up and down by my Lord Cornwallis, of silver.'

Pepys did not manage to catch any of the silver medals himself and because of the tumultuous noise he could barely make out the music. But as a chronicler conscious of his obligations, he had a bigger problem. The ceremony was still in full swing but he just had to go.

'I had so great a lust to **** that I went out a little while before the King had done all his ceremonies,' he confessed, 'and went round the Abbey to Westminster Hall, all the way within rayles, and 10,000 people, with the ground covered with blue cloth; and scaffolds all the way.'

With entirely untypical modesty Pepys doesn't fill in the word here. Perhaps he guessed his 23 April entry would one day be scrutinised for its unique record of the day the Restoration ceremonially began. He has fewer scruples elsewhere in his diary, noting for instance on 28 December 1664 that: 'I waked in the morning about 6 o'clock and my wife not come to bed; I lacked a pot, but there was none, and bitter cold, so was forced to rise and piss in the chimney, and to bed again.'

Chamber pots were always going missing or being spilled in Pepys' life. Or, indeed, turning up underneath his lady friends. It may be his compelling descriptions of the great London plague and fire that have made him famous, but his excruciating embarrassment on stumbling upon his friend Lady Sandwich in the middle of relieving herself in his dining room in Seething Lane is not easily forgotten either.

'I perceive by my dear Lady blushing that in my dining-room she was doing something upon the pott, which I also was ashamed of,' Pepys scribbled afterwards, no doubt mopping his brow. The pair had then attempted a ghastly conversation about a House of Commons debate on a Dutch war, in which they both doubtless tried to pretend that one of them was not heavily pregnant and sitting on a chamber-pot. The discourse, wrote Pepys, was 'without pleasure, through very pity to my Lady'.

His own relationship with the pot interests him in the way you might expect of a man who, like Martin Luther, suffered from kidney stones[*]. These crystalline obstructions cause considerable pain, an irresistible urge to urinate and frequent difficulty in succeeding.

In 1658 Pepys was operated on (restrained, in the absence of anaesthesia, by ropes and four strong men) to remove a stone as large as a tennis ball – an event which, while painful, delivered such relief that he resolved to celebrate it every year afterwards. The trouble recurred, however. After Pepys' death in 1703, a post-mortem found his left kidney completely ulcerated, his bladder gangrenous and seven stones lying around, weighing a total of four and a half ounces.

No wonder the poor man was obsessed with peeing.

Picasso

PABLO PICASSO EXPERIMENTED with everything, so it is not a huge surprise to learn that he assiduously watered his sculptures with urine. But oxidising a bronze that way can sometimes go wrong, as the Spanish master discovered when he set about trying to turn a bust of his mistress Dora Maar a subtly weathered green.

Craftsmen had been using urine to speed up the formation of a bluish-green patina on metals like copper (of which bronze is an alloy) for thousands of years[**]. Picasso was keen to see how it would work. Dora Maar, dark-haired muse for some of his most striking art during the eight years she shared his bed, found it hilarious.

See: Luther[*]
     Verdigris[**]

'So you don't know how Picasso patinated my bust?' she laughed when the photographer Brassaï (pseudonym of the Hungarian Gyula Halász) asked her some time later. 'Well, he peed on it,' she said. 'And for several days in a row. Maybe he was embarrassed to tell you.'

Unfortunately, as she went on to tell Brassaï, Picasso had overdone the oxidising. 'The result was disastrous. The bronze turned completely green, but an appalling green.'

Maar, who remained hurt at having been sidelined in 1943 by another of Picasso's many lovers, added wistfully: 'And to think that it happened to a bust of me in particular.'

Picasso, who also persuaded his children to pee on his sculptures, was not alone in practising the technique. The French sculptor Aristide Maillol used to water the large statues in his garden every day for the same reason. Maillol told Brassaï that rather than relieve himself in Paris, he often held on until he could make it back to his studio in nearby Marly-le-Roi, in order 'to save this precious elixir for his bronzes'. In the seventies Andy Warhol adopted the same technique in America*.

The head of Dora Maar is a powerful, rock-like piece which, in typical Picasso fashion, makes no concessions to the fine-featured beauty of the model. No wonder she was irked at being turned violently green as well.

𝔓isse-𝔓rophets

IN 1637 AN Essex MP by the name of Thomas Brian laid into the abusers of urine-inspection with a title that got straight to the point: *The Pisse-Prophet, Or, Certaine Pisse-Pot Lectures.* The title-page of his diverting treatise promised to lay bare the 'fallacies, deceit, and jugling of the pisse-pot science, used by all those (whether quacks and empiricks, or other methodicall physicians) who pretend knowledge of diseases, by the urine, in giving judgement of the same'.

See: 𝔄ndy 𝔚arhol*

There were a lot of quacks around by then, bringing the practice of inspecting urine to diagnose disease into disrepute[*]. Early exponents of uroscopy had tended to be circumspect: Isaac the Jew, a tenth-century physician and philosopher from Tunisia, warned that diagnosis should be limited to diseases of the liver and urinary passages.

But as uroscopy spread, other diseases were added. To the fury of serious practitioners, it became more of a witchcraft than a science, the butt of jibes and satire. Early sceptics included a woman who sent her doctor, a Master Giles of Stafford, a urine sample which consisted of her own urine mixed with that of her cow. Just to test him out, she said.

Monkeys with urine flasks began appearing in the borders of manuscripts and stained glass windows. These were supplanted in the late fifteenth century by grimmer images of skeletons inspecting the flasks[**]. As plague ravished Europe, urine-inspection was increasingly seen as a futile precursor to death.

In 1652 herbalist Nicholas Culpeper satirised the quacks in *The English Physitian*. In it a doctor pretends to be able to tell from a bottle of urine exactly how many stairs a patient has fallen down.

The quackery coincided with a growing intellectual realisation that the medieval system was inadequate for a proper understanding of disease. Henry VIII's physician, Thomas Linacre, a founder of the College of Physicians of London, tried to stop doctors using urine analysis as their sole method of diagnosis. And in his seventeenth-century treatise *Of Urines*, the physician Thomas Willis lambasted those 'Medicasters and Quacks' who 'behold the Urine sent in a Glass, shake it a little, and presently give Judgement'. Willis's recognition of other ways of inspecting urine – such as distillation, evaporation and precipitation – foreshadowed later chemical analysis.

So Thomas Brian's diatribe against the 'pisse-prophets' was a

---

See: Uroscopy[*]
          Jordan[**]

sign of the times. The world was changing and a coherent system[*]
had been stretched beyond its limit and then corrupted by
scoundrels. Brian reserved his strongest fire for practitioners who
didn't feel it necessary even to see the patient, instead picking up
clues from the messenger who had brought the sample and using
their own knowledge of disease to pronounce a diagnosis. The only
thing these men ever saw in urine, it seems, was their own profit.

𝔓liny

WHEN GAIUS PLINIUS Secundus was found dead under a heap of
pumice from the eruption of Mount Vesuvius in AD 79, the Roman
empire lost a breathtakingly well-informed polymath. Pliny the
Elder knew about everything. In his *Naturalis Historia*, published in
the last two years of his life, he produced an astonishing
encyclopaedic survey of ancient knowledge. Among its 20,000
facts, compiled (he boasted) from 2,000 books and 100 authors,
he explains how the Roman world used urine.

A recorder of received wisdom rather than a first-hand
investigator, Pliny passes on with lively enthusiasm the ailments he
had heard that urine could treat. Here are a few of them:

❖ **Sunburn.** Urine applied for two hours with the white of an ostrich
   egg.
❖ **Baby rashes and ulcers.** Old urine added to the ash of burnt
   oyster-shells.
❖ **Giant centipede bites.** Urine applied to the top of the head.
❖ **Skin irritation, sores on the head, dandruff and spreading
   genital ulcers.** Urine as a lotion. ('Nothing better,' says Pliny.)
❖ **Snake-bites, sore eyelids, pus and worms in the ear.** The urine of
   pre-pubescent children ('if boiled down to one half with a headed
   leek in new earthenware').
❖ **Pitted sores, burns, affections of the anus, chaps and scorpion
   stings.** Urine applied to the skin.

See: 𝔘roscopy[*]

❖ **Dog bites.** 'Each person's own urine, if it be proper for me to say so, does him the most good if a dog-bite is immediately bathed in it.'

What with snakes, scorpions, ear-worms, sunburn, centipedes and aggressive dogs, Pliny's recommendations certainly evoke the hazards of Roman life. The urine treatments sound fanciful but to an extent they anticipate scientific discoveries about the healing qualities of urea by nearly 2,000 years[*].

The *Natural History* was the last book Pliny published before his death at the age of 56 in the lethal fall-out from Vesuvius. Ever hungry for knowledge, he had sailed too close to the eruption. 'Fortune favours the bold,' he declared as he urged his helmsman across the Bay of Naples towards the erupting mountain.

𝔓ounding the 𝔚aste 𝔏and

ALTHOUGH ITS DISJOINTED style, cryptic allusions and strange, multiple voices baffled many early readers, *The Waste Land* is now hailed as perhaps the greatest English poem of the last hundred years. But the version T.S. Eliot published in 1922 had been heavily edited by his friend Ezra Pound. Some of Pound's slashing edits rescued the underlying music of the piece but his social delicacy about urination cost us two lines the poem really needed.

Pound, no mean poet himself, had returned Eliot's original manuscript with a raft of revisions. These ranged from losing a 'the' or inserting a 'who' here and there, to the culling of entire passages. The two urinary lines that never saw the light of day had fleshed out one of the most memorable scenes, in which the 'young man carbuncular' makes his way out after a perfunctory assignation with the lethargic typist. In Eliot's original version, he

Bestows one final patronising kiss,
And gropes his way, finding the stairs unlit;

_____
See: 𝔖kin[*]

And at the corner where the stable is,
Delays only to urinate, and spit.

Pound scored out the second couplet with the explanatory scribble 'probaly [sic] over the mark'. And Eliot took heed. In the published poem the young man is abruptly abandoned by his creator on the unlit stairs. The scene shifts back to the typist, reflecting that she's glad that's over.

Pound's sense of propriety ruined the rhyming sequence of *kiss* and *is*, and *unlit* and *spit*. It also denied us another telling detail of an evening of bored congress in the modern waste land.

Mind you, the deletion probably spared Eliot some embarrassment when he had to read the poem aloud to the royal family during the war. As the Queen Mother famously confided at a dinner party long afterwards: 'We had this rather lugubrious man in a suit, and he read a poem … I think it was called *The Desert*. At first the girls [princesses Elizabeth and Margaret] got the giggles and then I did and then even the King.'

Who knows what hilarity might have been unleashed if the spotty clerk had defiled a wall on his way out.

"Q"

A GADGET WIZARD will exploit anything that comes to hand. And Charles Fraser-Smith, the English intelligence officer immortalized by Ian Fleming as James Bond's quartermaster Q, was the best in the business. During the Second World War his job was to supply gizmos to secret agents in the field and POWs trying to escape. When casting around for something to make invisible ink reappear, he hit on urine.

Fraser-Smith, whose cover job was as an apparently boring civil servant in the clothing department of the Ministry of Supply, had been charged with providing route-maps for agents on the run. He managed to squirrel exquisite miniature maps into the bowls of smokers' pipes inside a cunning lining of fire-proof asbestos (which must have played havoc with the spies' lungs). But the larger ones really taxed his ingenuity. Reflecting that even German prison guards blew their noses, he opted finally to print the maps on innocent-looking pocket handkerchiefs.

He tested several types of invisible ink before discovering one that would not suddenly, and dangerously, reveal itself on being held up to the light or moistened. Then he looked for a substance that would develop the ink easily but was unlikely to be applied by accident. Urine, he explained later, was 'a choice I thought highly sensible, since that liquid was seldom likely to be in short supply'. When the secret agent needed to figure out where he was, he only had to pull out his handkerchief and pee on it for the layout of the local area to be miraculously revealed.

These urine-maps were only one of an extraordinary range of devices that gadget-mad Fraser-Smith produced for Special Operations Executive agents in occupied Europe. They included shaving brushes containing film, miniature cameras inside cigarette lighters, tunic buttons hiding an explosive charge, steel shoelaces that doubled as a thin saw and a used match containing a magnetised needle that could be casually dropped in a puddle to serve as a compass. Plans to give escapees concealed tablets of concentrated garlic-flavoured chocolate, to ensure an authentically continental breath, were abandoned. But the 'wee maps', as Fraser-Smith called the handkerchiefs, were among his most effective inventions.

On the subject of invisible ink it's worth noting that as well as developing it, urine can be used to make the ink itself. Dip your pen in, write a message and the words can be revealed later by applying heat. The urine is turned brown through a process of oxidisation.

Queen Boudicca

IN THE 1995 movie *Braveheart*, Mel Gibson's face was dyed a fetchingly anachronistic shade of blue. As the medieval Scottish patriot William Wallace, Mel's job was to scare the English. Mostly he scared the historians. But Scotland's football and rugby supporters immediately borrowed the blue-faced look, and nobody bothered that it went out of fashion about 300 years before Wallace was born and was more likely the badge of a southern queen.

Well, Scottish romantics must take encouragement where they can, but there's one detail that might genuinely shake them up: that blue dye was made with urine. It is Boudicca, a queen of the Iceni tribes in what is now East Anglia, who is remembered for leading her warriors against the occupying Roman army with their faces dyed blue. The dye was made from woad leaves fermented in urine to release the pigment*. Julius Caesar, who had led the Roman invasion back in 55 BC, thought the practice a piece of theatre to frighten his lads. 'All the British colour themselves with woad, making themselves the more terrifying in battle,' he wrote.[28]

It's now thought the face-painting may have had more to do with sensible health precautions than trying to look fierce. Woad was valued for its antiseptic properties, as was urine itself. It's argued that the early Britons might have been treating their skin pre-emptively to help heal the wounds of battle.

It's a medicine they will undoubtedly have needed, since the historian Tacitus reports that 80,000 of them fell in the great battle that ended Boudicca's rebellion and secured Roman control of the province.

Quenching

PEOPLE CLAIMED IT could split a feather in mid-air and stay razor-sharp through many a battle. Forged from Damascus steel, the richly patterned Damascene sword was legendary. It was said to be so flexible that a man could bend it right around his waist, yet hard enough to slash through almost any target. The crusading Richard the Lionheart was reported to be deeply impressed when his Muslim rival Saladin threw a silk pillow in the air and, with a flash of that curved blade, sliced it into ribbons as it fell.

But what was its secret? The armourers of Damascus hugged the mystery to themselves, laughing off suggestions that they quenched the sword in dragon's blood or magical chicken droppings. But medieval European blacksmiths liked to think the sword owed its power to their own method of quenching metal in urine.

Steel is an alloy of iron with, mainly, carbon. It had been quenched (the term used for the rapid cooling of red-hot metal) in all sorts of ways since ancient times. The effect was memorably described by Homer in *The Odyssey,* as early as 800 BC, in the unforgettable image of the great single eye of the giant Cyclops 'sizzling', when Odysseus and his men drive a stake into it, 'as a

---

See: Woad*

blacksmith plunges a glowing ax or adze / in an ice-cold bath and the metal screeches steam / and its temper hardens'.

If Homer's ice-cold bath contained a drop or two of pee, he never said so. But in the twelfth century Theophilus Presbyter, a German monk with expertise in glass and metal-working, made it clear that by his time urine had become one of the main quenchants. In his collection *On Various Arts*, Theophilus describes hardening tools by smearing them in pig fat and covering them with strips of goatskin and clay, then heating them red-hot before cooling them in urine.

The idea was to get the iron to absorb a little carbon evenly from the goatskin. Theophilus reckoned that urine – especially that of a small red-headed boy – gave tools a harder tempering than ordinary water. (These red-haired boys keep popping up through the ages in recipes involving urine. Perhaps high levels of the reddish pigment pheomelanin affected the quality of the urine. Or perhaps it was always just an old wives' tale, repeated with confidence as the red-haired mystique grew.) More mundanely, Theophilus also recommended the urine of goats fed on ferns for three days.

In 1558 the Italian scholar Giambattista della Porta described what he understood to be the underlying principle in his tome *Natural Magic*: 'If you quench red-hot iron in distilled vinegar, it will grow hard. The same will happen if you do it into distilled urine by reason of the salt.'

Different kinds of animal pee came to be tried in one recipe or another. Some blacksmiths favoured sheep urine. In more recent times the Metropolitan Museum of Art in New York was contacted about a sword owned by a Pakistani family for generations, which had been quenched in donkey urine.

Metallurgists today pour cold water on all the urine favourites. In fact, they say cold water is precisely all that's needed to quench hot steel. Good hardening, they say, is more likely to be down to carbon content or methods of heating than the medium by which the metal is quenched.

But you never know. Medieval armourers knew their stuff when it came to the art of weaponry. Just as the stained glass masterpieces of the medieval age are monuments to an enlightened use of urine[*], so we probably shouldn't be too patronising about the way the great swords of battle were being forged around the same time.

See: **Stained Glass**[*]

Rabelais

IT IS NOT a shock to find François Rabelais having fun with urine. Although the French author was also a learned monk, physician and humanist, his name became a byword for exuberant preoccupation with sex and excretion.

Gargantua and Pantagruel, Rabelais' rambling series of novels about the adventures of a pair of father and son giants, is a verbally extravagant satire on sixteenth-century French society and ecclesiastical power. The first book finds Gargantua *père* in Paris, so pestered by gaping citizens that he takes refuge by scaling the towers of Notre-Dame. To get his own back on the townspeople, he sends them screaming for the hills with a veritable tsunami of urine. It's a scene credited with giving Jonathan Swift the idea for his hero's more kindly effort in Lilliput[*].

As Rabelais recounts: 'With a smile [Gargantua] undid his magnificent codpiece and, bringing out his john-thomas, pissed on them so fiercely that he drowned two hundred and sixty thousand, four hundred and eighteen persons, not counting the women and small children.'

See: **Gulliver's Travels**[*]

Rabelais' books were widely read and in every sense outrageously successful. Free-thinking to the end, his last words before he died in 1553 were: 'I go to seek a Great Perhaps.' Churchmen of the day would have said there was no 'perhaps' about where the iconoclastic Rabelais was headed. His books, in all their excretory glory, not only managed to get themselves banned by the Roman Catholic Church but also attracted the personal denunciation of the Protestant reformer John Calvin.

Rats

REPORTED RAT INFESTATIONS are on the rise in the UK, up fifteen per cent in 2008 on the previous year to nearly 380,000 cases — an increase the National Pest Technicians Association blames on fortnightly bin collections and poorly secured household waste. However, it's not the bite of the rat you have to fear but its urine. Rats wash themselves rigorously. They are most scrupulous about this, bless their little clean paws. But without sphincter muscles they can't help constantly leaking. The urine they leave everywhere can carry diseases like salmonella, TB and Weil's disease.

It might be worth checking your face-cloth.

Recycling Trip

WHEN POLICE IN Anderson County, Tennessee, seized 241 two-litre bottles and 17 one-gallon jugs of urine in a raid in 2007, they began to realise how desperate some drug users must be. It was their third bust of a so-called 'pee lab', and the biggest so far. The urine had been deposited by methamphetamine users, who were trading it for the meth being manufactured in the house from older consignments.

Only ten to twenty per cent of methamphetamine passes unchanged into urine, compared to sixty per cent of Ecstasy and eighty-five per cent of the psychoactive ingredient in magic mushrooms*. So it would have taken at least a full day's worth of

See: **Santa Claus**[*]

urine to recapture a decent dose. In the lab the urine was 'cooked down' to filter the drug out.

One of the Anderson County sheriff's officers reported that meth users in jail – where at least one of the busted lab-technicians swiftly found himself – were often notably popular. Other inmates would 'process it and consume the urine to get a high off it,' said Lt Kenny Sharp. Slopping-out must have been interesting.

Revelation

THE BIBLE HAS little to say about urine, for which many will be profoundly grateful. Although the English urine therapist John Armstrong hailed a verse in Proverbs as divine guidance[*], the injunction, 'Drink waters from thy own cistern, flowing water from thy own well' is more likely to be a poetic way of urging husbands not to stray.

Robin Hood

EVERYONE KNOWS THAT England's favourite outlaw wore Lincoln green, the perfect camouflage for flitting among the trees in Sherwood Forest, bow and arrow at the ready. But what the ballad-writers failed to draw attention to is the secret ingredient that gave Robin Hood's tunic its special hue.

Lincoln, where the cloth was made, was a wealthy medieval woollen centre renowned for making the best greens in England. First of all the fabric was coloured a strong blue with a dye made from the popular woad plant. The woad was fermented in urine, the dyer's friend, to produce the blue pigment[**]. Then the cloth was dyed again, this time with yellow from mignonette. The result was Robin's famous leafy Lincoln green.

Of course it was hardly designer wear. Every yeoman for miles around, not to mention Robin's entire band of merrie men, wore those urine-dyed greens; even a chap on the side of the poor might be forgiven for thinking it was just a little common. So for special

---

See: Drinking It[*]

     Woad[**]

occasions, as one of the ballads reminds us, our man liked to dress up:

> He cloathed his men in Lincoln green
> And himself in scarlet red.[29]

Lincoln scarlet, for which the town was also famous, was made with an imported dye-stuff known as kermes, from the cochineal insect native to the Mediterranean. It was more expensive than Lincoln green, and in 1198 the Sheriff of Lincoln is recorded as parting with a hefty £30 for ninety ells (about 113 yards).

So where did a penniless outlaw like Robin Hood get *his* red outfit? Not being above a spot of pilfering from the rich, might he have relieved that very sheriff of his fancy cloth to brighten up his own pee-green wardrobe? There must be a ballad in it somewhere.

Rolling Stones

BEING IN POSSESSION of what a fellow Rolling Stone has called 'one of the biggest bladders in human existence', Bill Wyman was in a hurry to empty it. Along with Mick Jagger, Brian Jones and a few others he rushed from their Daimler into the Francis Service Station in Forest Gate, east London, and asked if he could use the toilet. It was March 1965 and the Rolling Stones' fledgling bad-boy career was about to get an unexpected boost.

Wyman, their bass guitarist, was told that the public toilet was out of order and he couldn't use the private one. In fact, said a mechanic, eyeing the eight or nine youngsters warily, would they all mind removing themselves from the premises immediately.

Lead singer Mick Jagger was having none of that. He gave the hapless mechanic the sort of brisk message that a pop star likes to be able to summon at will. 'We'll piss anywhere, man.' The others all chanted it after him. One of them capered around the forecourt. Wyman, Jagger and Jones then made good the boast against a wall of the garage.

'The car drove off with people inside sticking their hands through the windows in a well-known gesture,' said the prosecutor

Mr Kenneth Richardson frostily when the case came to trial that July. Fining Jagger, Wyman and Jones £5 each, the presiding magistrate could never have guessed what golden publicity he was ensuring with his stern admonition: 'You have been found guilty of behaviour not becoming of young gentlemen.' With these words the band's image was sealed.

From the moment they were found guilty of urinating against the wall of that petrol station, the Rolling Stones never looked back.

Romans

THE ROMANS NEEDED a seriously good detergent to wash the grime of Italy out of all those light-coloured tunics and sweeping woollen togas. They knew about soap but don't seem to have made it themselves. Instead, it was urine that kept Roman clothes as clean as their well-bathed owners.

There was no shortage of it swilling about in ancient Rome – as often as not descending from on high, as residents of high-rise apartments emptied their chamber-pots into disease-ridden streets. The *fullones*, professional cleaners who took in washing and bequeathed us the word 'fuller' (a scourer of cloth) made a useful contribution to public hygiene by collecting much of it in big terracotta jars placed near laundries. They also valued camel urine when they could get it, a particularly concentrated and potent detergent.

The use of urine in this way was embedded in the very language. No longer known as *urina*, in this incarnation it became the Latin *lotium* (literally, washing-up liquid). Inside the *fullonica* the fullers poured it into a series of large basins and soaked their customers' laundry in it, along with some 'fuller's earth' (*creta fullonica*), a mineral with powerful grease-dissolving properties found all over the Mediterranean. (Later in the process the togas of election candidates were rubbed with a special type of *creta* to make them shining white.)

For the next stage of cleaning, the clothes were put in tubs in small booths divided by low walls, where the fullers performed an extraordinary manoeuvre described by the writer Seneca as the *saltus fullonicus* – the fuller's leap. Leaning against the walls for support, they jumped up and down on the soaking garments to work the urine in and every vestige of dirt and grease out. Tunics hitched to the knees, the fullers (usually lowly freedmen or working slaves) danced and leaped and stamped in the urine for hours at a time.

Smelly and exhausting, it was an unenviable job. Like the dyers of the Middle Ages[*], Roman fullers were roundly despised for doing dirty work with beautiful results. In the unforgiving pages of Roman satire they crop up regularly in the company of other morally questionable professionals like cobblers, innkeepers, bath-keepers, bakers, blacksmiths and weavers.

The fullers laughed all the way to the bank, though. Their work was so commercially lucrative that one enterprising emperor popped a tax on the urine they collected[**]. And although the ammonia fumes must have made the *fullonica* an unhealthy place to work, the historian Pliny the Elder reckoned that immersing your legs in urine every day was good for one thing at least. 'Men's urine relieves gout,' he wrote in his *Natural History*, 'as is shown by the testimony of fullers, who for that reason never, they say, suffer from this malady.'[***]

Collecting the urine in unglazed and porous terracotta jars had its hazards, though. If a fuller was stingy enough to put out a cracked one, the contents could spill everywhere, leaving a smell so bad that the Latin satirist Martial wrote of it to evoke repellent body odour. The woman Thais, he sneered, smelled worse than a belching lion, worse than a randy goat, worse than a dead dog – and definitely worse than 'the old jar of a penny-pinching fuller recently broken in the middle of the road'.[30]

Unappreciated as they might have been, fullers were nonetheless the master-chemists of ancient Rome. They harnessed

---

See: Blue Monday[*]
       Vespasian[**]
       Pliny[***]

the laws of nature to keep Rome gleaming white. And their methods stood the test of time: the amazing pee-dance was still being performed in the Scottish Hebrides at the end of the twentieth century*.

See: Harris Tweed

Santa Claus

IT'S NOT THE way we like to see the old cove but it seems Santa Claus may have started life as a red-faced Siberian shaman. According to this theory, Santa drank urine as a way of recycling the delights of magic mushrooms. He also herded intoxicated reindeer whose pee was equally good for a sly tipple.

The theory has been proposed, quite seriously, because the semi-nomadic people of Siberia and Lapland used to be keen on eating the *amanita muscaria* (or fly agaric) mushroom for its hallucinogenic qualities. Because some eighty-five per cent of its major psychoactive compound is not metabolized in the body, these northern tribesmen could experience the trip again and again through drinking their own – and other people's – urine.

One effect of the mushroom, as Santa Claus would know, was a sensation of flying. Another reported by Victorian travellers was a perception of size distortion known as macropsia. (That thought may have been behind Alice's mushroom-eating in Lewis Carroll's *Alice in Wonderland*, which makes her grow alternately very tall and very small.)

Explorers in Siberia reported that the reindeer were also partial to the mushrooms and would prance about drunkenly under the influence. The urine of these tripped-out reindeer was itself popular to drink for its psychedelic effects.

It's not hard to see how the Santa Claus figure, a keen traveller by reindeer, could raise speculation. Is his ruddy glow the tell-tale flush of the mushroom-eater? Is his jolly 'Ho, ho, ho' the euphoria of a magic urine drinker? Might his red and white fur-trimmed coat and black boots be mimicking the typical garb of mushroom harvesters, out collecting with their sacks? Could his propensity for clambering down chimneys reflect the shaman's habit of climbing through the smoke-hole in his reindeer-hide yurt that also served as the front door? It all sounds vaguely plausible.

But it's doubtful if Santa Claus would have looked quite so healthy if he had really been consuming fly agaric mushrooms (which are not, incidentally, the *psilocybe* variety that modern thrill-seekers now know as magic mushrooms). The red fly agaric toadstool with white dots, the kind beloved of fairy-tale illustrators, is potentially deadly, inducing a range of symptoms from nausea and delirium to brain damage. Perhaps it's just as well that so many of the trips were experienced through the weaker medium of urine.

It's disappointing to have to report, however, that there has been some debunking of the Santa theory. In 1996 historian Ronald Hutton spoiled the Christmas party by pointing out that Siberian shamans did not travel by sleigh, wear red and white coats, or climb out of smoke holes in the roofs of yurts.[31]

Still, there's no getting round the fact that Santa Claus does have a very red face and every appearance of enjoying himself.

Shampoo

WHEN THE DANISH explorer Peter Freuchen went to live in Greenland for several years at the beginning of the twentieth century, he married an Inuit woman, had two children and freely adopted native ways. But one aspect of the culture he was not so keen on was the Inuit habit of washing their hair in urine. Freuchen said he was appalled by the smell of ammonia from his companions' tresses.

Perhaps they didn't rinse the urine out properly afterwards. Today, elderly people far beyond Greenland still remember using it in their hair and never mention a smell afterwards. In many parts of rural Europe cow's urine was the shampoo of choice. In the Scottish Highlands there are people who recall collecting a bucket-load from the byre as children and rubbing their hair in it. 'It gave it such a lovely sheen,' they tell you blithely. Older country folk in Iceland also praise the ability of cow urine to cut through grease and leave locks clean and shiny.

Urine therapists today are trying to reintroduce the old rural habits. They recommend massaging urine briskly into the scalp, leaving it for up to an hour (while you do what exactly?) and then rinsing it out with lukewarm water. If you don't rinse it, the hair is said to be even more lustrous, though presumably tending to the Inuit effect. They also suggest a mixture of potato and sulphur powder mixed with heated, stale urine to slow down hair loss.

Shewee

THINK, GIRLS, ABOUT the thistles and nettles that lurk in the twilight shadows beyond every idyllic camping spot. Think about the ungainly squat and the paranoid conviction that someone is watching you. Think about the trying business of keeping your shoes dry and the wearisome queues for grubby outdoor cubicles.

Product designers like Sam Fountain have thought of little else. In 1999 she patented the Shewee, an elegantly fluted plastic funnel which she later launched on a softly tittering world from her base in Surrey. Even after a publicity boost from the BBC's *Dragon's Den*, it took time to make its mark. She explains: 'It's such a shocking product. Like tampons, at first. We had to wait for it to sell itself.'

Fountain found her market among female campers, hikers and climbers, with a sideline in medical sales to sex-change patients and an extra boost from revellers during the music festival season. You can even choose your colour of funnel: with an eye on the places where women may find themselves on active military service, army girls in a hurry arc targeted with Desert Sand and Nato Green.

From her office in Walton-on-the-Hill, Fountain now employs five full-time staff and has an annual turnover of £250,000. Accessories include 'X-fronts' – pink knickers with a discreet fly in the front to slip a funnel through – and a 15cm extension pipe for multiple layers of clothing.

'I used it myself on the London to Brighton bicycle ride,' she bubbles. 'You just open your fly, push your underwear to one side, poke it through and you're away. I found it really liberating.'

Women who fancy this particular form of liberation are now spoiled for choice. Should they go for Fountain's hard-wearing Shewee? Or would they prefer the more pliable Whizz Freedom? How about the bendy polyethylene TravelMate? Or the American (naturally) My Sweet Pee shield? Marketed by retired twin sisters from Houston, Texas, this one is perfumed with citrus and comes with a flat piece of rubber as a splash guard along with, as the advert puts it, 'a trough'. As one of the sisters trills brightly, 'It's a wonderful little stocking filler.'

Female empowerment is the mantra of urinary device marketing. 'Stand up and take control,' they urge you. But scratch the surface of pee liberation and you discover a more coy truth. 'At least when you're going this way,' says the inventor of the Shewee, 'no-one can see your bottom.'

Skin

DUTCHMAN COEN VAN der Kroon was helping to pull a cart up the side of a mountain in India, when a large stone was knocked loose from a wall and fell a full metre on to the middle toe of his left foot. It ripped off the nail and surrounding flesh right to the bone. After a week the whole toe was so infected that locals warned him about gangrene. At that point he was advised to wind a cloth soaked in his own urine around the toe, which, with some revulsion, he did.

'After three days the wound was completely clean, the swelling was gone and the pain considerably reduced,' van der Kroon reports in his book *The Golden Fountain*. 'On the fourth day, radiant, new, pink skin appeared under the wound tissue. A few days thereafter, the wound was almost completely healed and a new nail had even started to grow.'

He has been evangelising the medicinal benefits of both urine and Indian religious practices ever since. But you don't need to follow the urine therapists down their more febrile byways* to acknowledge both a long history of anecdotal reports that urine is good for the skin and a more recent history of clinical investigation that might explain it.

The Greek philosopher Aristotle rubbed urine into his scalp to counter baldness. The Roman author Pliny swore by its efficacy in treating burns, ear pus, rashes and head-sores**. The Aztecs used it to clean wounds. Mongolian horse warriors washed themselves in it to combat crotch rot. Native Americans in New England treated ant and snake bites with it, while a tribe encountered in 1806 by Lewis and Clark's expedition to Oregon had the custom 'of bathing themselves all over with urine every morning'.

Fishermen the world over have sworn by its antiseptic qualities for cuts from knives and fish-hooks. Soldiers on the battlefield have peed on wounds, convinced it would help protect them from infection. In fact, by the time urine was being used as an emergency antiseptic in the First World War, scientists had already started to show why it was so effective. In 1906 the pathologist W. James Wilson was one of a number of medical researchers to demonstrate that its prime component, urea, available in synthetic form since 1828,*** could inhibit the growth of micro-organisms.

Then in 1915 two military doctors, W. Symmers and T.S Kirk, published a seminal study on their treatment of wounded soldiers in the Ulster Volunteer Force Hospital. All the patients had been treated with urea, they reported, and it had been found that infected wounds dressed with urea crystals once in twenty-four hours gave better results than similar cases treated in any other way.

See: Drinking It*
　　Pliny**
　　Vitalism***

In a 1938 edition of *The Lancet*, Leon Muldavis, senior casualty officer at London's Royal Free Hospital, along with his colleague Jean Holtzman at the London School of Medicine for Women, described the application of urea crystals to treat abscesses, infected traumatic wounds, infected haematomas, cellulitis, septic wounds from burns, varicose ulcers, carbuncles and inflamed tendons of the hand.

Later studies examined urea's dermatological effects. In 1992 Dr Gunnar Swanbeck in Sweden observed that urea had an anti-itching effect and helped in the treatment of intractable skin diseases like eczema and psoriasis. He reported that urea creams were useful for all degrees of dry skin, although they could sting.

The effectiveness of urea as a moisturiser is no secret to the cosmetics industry. It has been shown to minimise water loss, replenish the water content of the skin and increase its water-binding capacity. In some of the more excitable skincare websites, wrinkles themselves are conveniently banished by urea – anti-ageing claims which are disconcertingly close to those made for urine itself down the ages[*].

These days the synthetic version of urea, often known as carbamide, is found in a wide range of skin creams, facial cleansers and foundations, shampoos and conditioners, as well as in medical products like ear wax softeners and wound or burn ointments. Its growing reputation as a 'natural' agent means it is increasingly flaunted in skincare products promoted as healthy. It is also an ingredient in whitening toothpaste, which would greatly amuse the ancient tribes once mocked by the Romans for brushing their teeth in urine[**].

Those who promote the use of urine as a therapy urge us to apply urea from source and save our money. What they never quite understand is that some of us might prefer a jar of perfumed cream to a pot of pee.

See: Hinduism[*]
      Toothpaste[**]

Slavish Attention

IT HAS BEEN the unhappy lot of slaves and courtiers throughout history to find themselves in charge of chamber-pots. The more powerful the personage the more intimate the attentions demanded.

If the *Satyricon of Petronius* is to be believed, Roman slaves even had the daunting task of hopping around with a chamber-pot in the garden, trying to position it accurately while their master played ball. The novel describes a fabulously wealthy Roman called Trimalchio who had an agile eunuch standing by with a silver vessel as the balls flew past.

'Trimalchio snapped his fingers,' writes Petronius, 'and at the signal the eunuch held out the chamber-pot for him, without his ever stopping play.' A formidable feat on both sides.

Royalty has always expected assiduous attentions in this regard. Courtiers of James I of Great Britain had to grapple with a key to unlock his chamber-pot, which was encased in a leather box to deter tampering. England's Henry VIII opted for a 'close stool' padded in black velvet and trimmed with ribbons, fringes and quilting, which some minion had tacked together with 2,000 gilt nails.

Louis XIV of France took the nonsense to new heights by getting each of his 3,000 courtiers to bend a knee as his silver pot processed regally through the Palace of Versailles on its way to be emptied. It was almost as divine as he was. We're even told that courtiers jostled for the privilege of carrying this precious burden.

The Sun King himself was as fond of his chamber-pots as a chap who publicly underwent more than 2,000 enemas in the course of his reign would have to be – though he did have to have some of the silver melted down to help pay for his wars.

Smelling Salts

WHERE WOULD VICTORIAN literature be without smelling salts? Waved under the noses of swooning maidens and susceptible matrons overcome with fainting, *sal volatile* was a handy tool for arousing consciousness. Some police constables in Victorian Britain even carried a special container to revive fainting women.

What brings them round is a whiff of ammonium carbonate gas, which irritates the membranes of the nose and lungs, triggering an inhalation reflex. That compound is now made synthetically (as boxers, who are still brought round with it in the ring, will be glad to know). But it was originally derived from urine.

Organic nitrogen-containing material like hair, animal horn and decomposed urine were all common sources of ammonium carbonate. In fact, the shavings of deer horns and hooves were so popular for the purpose that smelling salts also became known as 'salt of hartshorn'.

In 1620 the self-educated Italian chemist Angelo Sala, whose experiments with silver salts laid the foundations of photography, synthesised the 'volatile salt of urine' (ammonium carbonate) with 'spirit of salt' (hydrochloric acid) to produce another of urine's most useful salts, ammonium chloride or *sal ammoniac* — which was particularly useful for cleaning metal surfaces before soldering.

Sal volatile itself is a substance that will forever be associated with Charles Dickens' gallery of overcome ladies. But it's worth remembering that ammonia, however it may be obtained, is a powerful gas. Whoever had the task of reviving those fading violets had to be careful not to put it too close to their own noses, as *Hard Times'* Mr Bounderby was well aware when he stepped into a chemist's shop to buy a bottle of the very strongest smelling salts. "'By George!" said Mr. Bounderby, "if she takes it in the fainting way, I'll have the skin off her nose, at all events!'"

Sniffing Cancer

AN ASTONISHING SCIENTIFIC trial has shown that dogs can sniff out bladder cancer in urine. The trained dogs' success rate in repeatedly identifying cancerous urine was 41%, compared with the 14% expected from chance alone. Convincing evidence that dogs can smell cancer.

For the study in Amersham[32], six dogs of varying breeds were taught to differentiate the scent of the urine of patients with bladder cancer from that of control specimens including water, normal urine, blood-flecked urine from menstruating women and urine from patients with non-malignant urological disease. The training proceeded with search-and-find games of increasing complexity.

It was not easy for the dogs. Researchers needed them to be able to recognise an odour signature for cancer from among the hundreds of others present in urine, without recourse to the 'pure' source to which they would have access if tracking, say, drugs or explosives.

But after seven months the dogs were ready to go. The trial, done nine times with different specimens, tested their ability to select one cancer sample from among six controls. Some dogs did better than others, but as a group they identified the urine sample containing positive bladder cancer on 22 out of 54 occasions. Researchers were delighted. If they can establish the exact chemical composition of the cancer signature, the next step is to develop a screening process for it.

But those six dogs have already helped at least one patient. During their training every one of them insisted on lying down beside a supposedly negative control sample. The consultant was so alarmed that he carried out tests on the donor at once and found evidence of undiagnosed kidney cancer.

Space

A 'URINE DUMP at sunset' is by all accounts more appealing than it sounds. According to Apollo 9 astronaut Russell Schweickart, who coined the phrase, the shower of tiny golden spheroids is the most beautiful sight in space.

'As the stuff comes out and hits the exit nozzle, it instantly flashes into ten million little ice crystals which go out almost in a hemisphere. Because, you know, you're exiting into essentially a perfect vacuum, and so the stuff goes in every direction. … It's really a spectacular sight.'

At least until urine recycling is perfected*, peeing into a hose which leads through a valve into the heavens remains the chief method of getting rid of urine in space. However, the operation is

---

See: **Wee Chefs***

fraught with hazard. Supposedly designed to work on female as well as male astronauts, the neck of the rubber hose manages to fit neither.

The vacuum is also suspect. Male Apollo astronauts have recalled ruefully that after the condom-like attachment on the end of the hose was rolled on, they had to time the opening of the spacecraft valve to perfection. Too soon, and the vacuum of space would begin to pull uncomfortably. Too late, and the pretty gold droplets would end up floating around inside the spacecraft.

While the urine show is enchanting, staging it inside is never advisable. When a bag of stored urine burst early in the Gemini 7 mission in 1965, the floating globules threatened to short out the spacecraft hardware (nowadays protected by an epoxy coating). Worse, the two astronauts never succeeded in collecting them all. Pilot Jim Lovell later described the voyage as 'two weeks in the men's room'.

Storing urine on board never proved more taxing than during the return to earth of Apollo 13, crippled by an explosion on its way to the moon in 1970. Using the lunar module as a space-lifeboat, the crew were easing their way back when Mission Control instructed them not to dump urine into space so as to avoid altering the homebound trajectory. The three astronauts then spent much of the flight home wondering where on earth, or off earth, to put it.

First they located three bags in the command module, then six small ones in the lunar module. After that they connected a Portable Life Support System condensate tank to a long hose, and drained urine into two large bags designed for another purpose altogether.

'I'm glad we got home when we did,' Commander Jim Lovell said later, 'because we were just about out of ideas for stowage.'

Sport

FOR THE GODS and goddesses of sport, urine testing is the embarrassing underbelly of divinity. It means private humiliation in the midst of public glory. One minute these household names are holding aloft a gleaming trophy or blinking mistily through a national anthem, the next they are peeing into a stranger's cup.

With urine testing on the frontline of an intensifying war against drug cheats, the squeeze on athletes is tightening. World Anti-Doping Agency rules, implemented by an increasing number of sporting bodies, dictate that top sportsmen and women have to log their whereabouts for one hour every day for the entire year, during which they can be followed into the toilet and watched. Most athletes accept the rules with good grace as the price of clean sport. But rebellion is spreading.

Spain's Rafael Nadal has called the procedures 'an intolerable hunt'. Britain's top tennis player Andy Murray complains the rules make it almost impossible to live a normal life. 'I got a visit at 7 a.m. one morning at my home, right after I had travelled home from Australia,' he grumbled. 'The official insisted on watching me provide a sample, literally with my trousers round my ankles, and then insisted that I wrote down my own address, even though he was at my private home at 7 a.m..'*

It's all part of an aggressive campaign by sporting authorities to keep ahead of drug cheats who are themselves becoming ever more inventive**. Even before the 2010 Winter Olympics began in Vancouver, thirty athletes were banned from competing after anti-doping violations, which may have included simply not making their whereabouts known for the required hour a day.

The 2,500 or so samples taken at those games eclipsed the 1,500 tests at Turin in 2006. Organisers of the London Games in 2012 intend to test a record 5,000 samples at the Olympics and 1,200 at the Paralympics. At 100ml a specimen, that will send 6,200 litres of pee hurtling around London during those three weeks. But even after testing, escape from the urine trap is by no means assured. Samples can now be frozen and stored for up to eight years, awaiting methods of detection that no-one has even developed yet.

The tightened observation procedures should at least prevent an enterprising cheat like the former American football star and

---

See: **Chaperones***
Whizzinator**

marijuana smoker Shawn King airily running rings around the system.

In his heyday King was subject to random testing from the National Football League up to ten times a month, even being tracked down once on a cruise ship. But his chaperone, who clearly needed to brush up on the guidelines[*], was lenient about actually watching him urinate. Spotting his chance, King refined a system of substituting 'clean' for 'dirty' urine, which involved building up a store during a season when he wasn't smoking for use during the times when he was. 'I saved up about 18 months' worth of urine in the carport,' he reports proudly.

Since he never knew when the 'pee guy' would pounce, King made sure he always packed a bottle of clean urine along with the shorts and sunglasses when he went on holiday. During the football season he poured it into pill bottles and condoms, which he embedded in the waistband of his trousers, ready for instant action. Knowing the NFL performed spot tests to make sure the fluid was at body temperature, he took other precautions too.

'I'd put it in the jacuzzi all night,' he grins. 'I'd get up in the morning, get it out of the jacuzzi, tape it to the vents in my truck and turn the heat on.'

The scam worked like a dream until King ran short of clean urine one day. He called a girlfriend and said he needed a favour. Could she send him some of her own so that he could make it through the next test? No problem. It arrived by Fed Ex as pristine as he could wish. There was only one hitch: 'I failed that test because I came up pregnant.'

Stained Glass

SIT IN ONE of the great Gothic cathedrals – Chartres, perhaps, or Canterbury – catching your breath at the jewelled light in the windows, silent with wonder at how those medieval craftsmen managed to create such lively pictorial power out of glass, and

See: **Chaperones**[*]

there's every chance your first thought is not going to be pee. But the artists who created Europe's stained glass masterpieces thought about it a lot. Urine helped to make their art.

The glass itself was made from sand and wood ash. For colours, metallic oxide chemicals were added into the molten mix: metals like cobalt, which gave the dazzling electric blues that make some of these windows look so uncannily modern, or copper for the rich rubies. To cut the glass, lines were drawn into it with a red-hot rod and urine was poured over these to make the glass fracture. The edges would be rounded off by a cutting tool, which itself had probably been tempered in urine[*].

Urine came into its own again when the glass was painted. It was the substance most commonly used to turn paint powder, made from finely ground pieces of glass, into a paste that could be applied to the surface of the glass. All the details that brought the biblical scenes or saintly stories alive for the unlettered folk gazing up at them – the lines on a face, the folds of a robe, the texture of hair, the bent fingers on a hand – are likely to have been painted on with pee.

The oldest window in Canterbury Cathedral, made around 1176 to depict Adam digging and delving with his spade in the garden of Eden, is an enchanting case in point. Perhaps it's time to rehabilitate the term 'piss artist'.

Survival

IT'S PROBABLY AS well that the American hiker Aran Ralston hadn't read the US Military's survival handbook on the day he trapped his arm under a boulder at the bottom of a Utah canyon and ran out of water. Marines are taught that drinking your own urine is a bad idea, but it kept Ralston alive.

The 28-year-old mechanical engineer was on a lone hiking trip in the Blue John Canyon in 2003, when a massive rock became dislodged and trapped him. For days he lay helpless at the bottom of a hole. He was a hundred feet down a gorge, twenty miles from

See: Quenching[*]

the nearest paved road and surrounded by hundreds of miles of uninhabited desert. His right arm was pinned under an 800-pound boulder.

With his water supplies running out, Ralston took the only action he could think of: he began to store urine in his empty hydration pack. He found the sight of it deeply uninviting. After four hours it had separated into layers: 'a viscous brown soup on the bottom, a dingy orange fluid in the middle, a clear golden liquid on top.' He said later it reminded him 'of the yeast in the bottom of a bottle of home-brewed beer – but substantially less appealing.'

But that was nothing to the taste of it. By next morning, water finished, Ralston tried his first sip. It tasted 'like hell'. By the following evening, four days into his ordeal, the 'grotesque stash' of urine was all that sustained him. It had 'eroded the inside of my mouth, leaving my palate raw, reminding me that I am going to die'.

Ralston knew the urine could not sustain him long. The next day, after five days of fruitlessly trying to lift and break the boulder, he managed to amputate his arm with the dull blade of a multi-use tool and staggered out of the canyon to safety. The arm was later retrieved by the park authorities, cremated and returned to its owner. He scattered the ashes back at the boulder.

By recycling the only liquid to hand, Aron Ralston was doing what adventurers have resorted to for centuries when survival is in jeopardy. When the Portuguese explorer Ferdinand Magellan's fleet of five ships ran out of water on their voyage around the world in 1519, his sailors took similar measures to tide them over until they could replenish supplies. One crewman, who had drunk a few nasty beverages in his time, damned it with faint praise: 'It was surprisingly not unsavoury, having no worse a taste than a flagon most foul with rancid port.'

In China two brothers trapped in a collapsed coal-mine in 2007 also had recourse to this foul brew. They survived on urine for six days before tunnelling their way out. 'You can only take small sips,' Meng Xiachen told the *Beijing News*. 'And when you've finished, you just want to cry.'

In January 2010, an emaciated man, so ghostly pale that his mother thought he was a corpse, was pulled alive from the rubble of his bedroom in the Haitian capital, Port-au-Prince – a full ten days after the catastrophic earthquake that killed around 170,000 people. Twenty-one-year-old Emmanuel Buso was one of the last people found alive before rescue efforts were called off. Doctors reported that he was in surprisingly good shape. He told them he had survived by drinking his own urine.

Some survival experts, notably the U.S. Military and the SAS, advise their soldiers against drinking urine because of the dehydrating effect of the high salt component. But when there is literally no other option, the 95% water content can at least expand your chances for another few days – which, as Emmanuel Buso proved, might just be long enough to make all the difference in the world.

However, experts say you can only recycle urine three or four times before it becomes so dangerously concentrated that drinking it causes symptoms similar to total kidney failure. 'At that point, you're doomed either way,' says a former marine cheerfully, 'from dehydration on the one hand or renal meltdown on the other.'

Swimming Pools

SHOPPERS ACROSS THE United States and Canada have tried to buy it, signs claiming its efficacy have been erected outside swimming baths and Orson Welles allegedly tricked pool-guests into believing it could expose their secret*. Despite that, no chemical has ever been discovered that can colour the water around a peeing swimmer.

There are so many other organic and inorganic compounds clinging to people's bodies – in sweat, sun-cream, cosmetics and soap residue – that a Nobel prize would be in the offing if you could develop a substance that reacted to urine alone. But even the rumour of such a dye has proved a powerful deterrent.

See: Orson Welles*

LIFE OF 𝒫EE   167

Professional signs ('Wee Alert' is a favourite) warning that a pool is being monitored by a chemical which will expose guilty swimmers with a humiliating cloud of red or blue dye, are said to keep a number of American adults on the straight and narrow. Children, whose criminal tendencies in this area are well attested, seem to be less impressionable.

The Scottish writer and broadcaster Tom Morton has confessed that it was a matter of childhood honour and survival to urinate immediately on entering Troon's freezing-cold outdoor swimming pool in the sixties: 'Peeing was essential, we all agreed, to prevent your willy falling off.' By the weekend the pool had been warmed up by 'hundreds of gallons of bodily fluids over the week, and the effect of whatever sun there had been. True, the water was by Saturday almost completely opaque, a dirty, cloudy green, but it enveloped you like amniotic fluid.'

No academic researcher is likely to get to the bottom, as it were, of how much of this goes on. Who, after all, is going to admit to letting go in a swimming pool? (One in five adults, according to one US poll.) However, by measuring potassium in the water, Heidelberg medical microbiologist Dr Lothar Erdinger has had a stab at calculating that an average of 77.5ml of urine is released per person into indoor pools. That's an espresso-sized cup for every swimmer.

Interestingly, although ammonia makes up a tiny 5% of the total nitrogen content of urine, much bigger concentrations are found in baths – formed, it appears, because of chemical reactions with chlorine. So arguably it's not the urine that's the problem, so much as the disinfectant.

It's worth remembering that in Iceland the continuously flowing, geothermally-heated outdoor pools have no filters or chemical sanitisers such as chlorine or bromine. Swimmers are forced – on pain of being sent packing – to shower thoroughly in the nude before they go near the pool. What they do in the water is their own business but they remain a healthy nation.

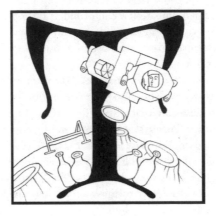

Terror

AN ENTIRE HERD of terrified cows losing control of their bladders, all at once, in the middle of the night, is awe-inspiring. It's a phenomenon that Maasai herdsmen understand all too well. It means a lion is about to strike.

Joseph Lemasolai Lekuton, a Harvard-educated teacher in Virginia, grew up among the semi-nomadic Maasai on the savannah of northern Kenya. At the age of fourteen he awoke in the night to a sound like gushing rain.

'I looked up. The starlight was gone, clouds were everywhere, and there was a drizzle falling. But that wasn't the sound. The sound was all of the cows starting to pee. All of them, in every direction. And that is the sign of a lion. A hyena doesn't make them do that. An elephant doesn't make them do that. A person doesn't. Only the lion. We knew right away that a lion was about to attack us.'[33]

The physiological explanation is straightforward enough. Extreme fear is known to trigger an involuntary relaxing of the sphincter muscles that control the flow of urine. We see it in puppies. They wet the floor so often in response to an angry word that dog manuals call it 'fear-urination' and urge patience with the toilet training.

En masse, this reflex action can produce a symphony of panic, the unforgettable expression of desperate animal fear. For the Maasai, urine will always be the sound of terror.

Testing Times

MORE THAN THREE thousand years before modern scientists hit on it, the ancient Egyptians had already figured out that urine was the key to detecting pregnancy. They watered some barley and emmer-wheat seeds for a few days with the urine of a woman who thought she might be pregnant. If these germinated at all, a baby was reckoned to be on the way. If only the barley thrived, the child was confidently expected to be male. If the wheat shot up, it would be a girl.

The practice was reported in the Greater Berlin Papyrus, dating from around 1300 BC, which was discovered by Heinrich Brugsch during excavations at Sakkara near Cairo. We can't know how many Egyptian women received a shock a few months after their pregnancy test but the theory is not without some credibility. When scientists tested it in 1963, they found the urine of pregnant women did promote growth seventy per cent of the time, perhaps because of elevated levels of oestrogens.

In Iceland they say that if a woman in past centuries wanted to know whether she was pregnant, she put a sewing needle at the bottom of a bowl of urine and left it lying there overnight. By the next morning, if the needle stayed shiny she was not thought to be pregnant; if she was expecting, she would find spots of rust on the needle. In this case scientists scratch their heads and suggest there would have been surprises aplenty in the following months.

It was animals, rather than needles or grains, that took the real brunt of the search for a modern pregnancy test. The key was identifying human chorionic gonadatropin (hCG) in urine, a hormone secreted by the placenta after the fertilized egg implants in the uterus. In 1927 the German scientists Selmar Aschheim and Bernhard Zondek tested for pregnancy by injecting a woman's urine into an immature rat. If the woman were pregnant, the rat would come into heat.

A later test by Maurice Friedman involved injecting urine into the ear veins of a female rabbit. Again, if hCG were present, the rabbit ovulated within forty-eight hours – a discovery for which the unfortunate animal paid with its life, since the effect could only be observed by killing it. At least when the British biologist Lancelot Hogben injected a female African clawed toad with urine in 1939, the creature could externally produce eggs to prove that the woman was pregnant.

Animals got a break after that, but pregnancy tests today are still based on registering the effects on a woman's urine of increased levels of hCG.

Toothpaste

THE ROMANS WERE extremely snooty about the way their uncouth Spanish neighbours, the Celtiberians, insisted on cleaning their teeth with urine. Bathing baby rashes and centipede stings in pee was perfectly acceptable to the Roman sensibility* but putting it your mouth was quite another.

In fact, the Romans felt so superior about the habit that they failed to see the irony in those urine-cleaned Celtiberian teeth being so much healthier than their own. The first-century poet Catullus penned a satirical poem about a Celtiberian called Egnatius, which captures the Roman sneer perfectly. Egnatius had the habit of smiling inappropriately. Spaniards like him, wrote Catullus, 'rub their teeth and red gums / every morning with what they have urinated, so that the cleaner your teeth are / the more urine you are shown to have drunk.'[33]

Catullus' superciliousness about clean teeth rings less smart today. Nor would his jibe have impressed the father of modern dentistry, Pierre Fauchard, who thought rinsing your mouth in urine an excellent idea for pain-relief and health**. Now that urea

---

See: 𝔓liny*
     Oral Rinse**

is commonly used as a teeth whitener[*], the Celtiberians are truly having the last, and pearliest, laugh.

Tragedy

AMONG THE TERRIBLE litany of mistakes that led London police hunting a terrorist to shoot dead an innocent Brazilian electrician in July 2005, the decision of a surveillance officer to relieve himself at exactly the wrong moment was the most tragically banal. Code-named Frank, he was one of a team staking out the block of flats where Hussain Osman, on the run with three others after unsuccessfully trying to blow up three tube trains and a London bus the previous day, was believed to live.

Frank was in a van watching the entrance to the flats in Tulse Hill and had a video camera on hand to film the suspect if he appeared. But the man who emerged into the street that summer's morning was not Hussain Osman, would-be suicide bomber, but 27-year-old Jean Charles de Menezes setting off for work.

Frank, on secondment to the Metropolitan Police from the armed forces, should have grabbed the camera at once. But at that moment he had been taken short. As Jean Charles stepped out of the front door, Frank was occupied inside the van urinating into a bottle. With only one hand free, he reached not for the camera but for his radio. Instead of snatching vital video footage, he was able to give his colleagues only a verbal description of the quarry.

His was far from the only failure in the inexorable sequence of events that cost Jean Charles de Menezes his life soon afterwards, shot seven times in the head at point-blank range as he boarded an underground train at Stockwell station. But it was perhaps the most heart-searingly human.

See: Skin[*]

Tranquillity Base

IT IS A sobering thought that four urine collection bags are currently littering the surface of the moon. They are among the hundred or so items left in 1969 by the first humans to land on the moon.

Apollo 11 astronauts Neil Armstrong and Buzz Aldrin dumped the equipment at Tranquillity Base just before they lifted off to rendezvous with the orbital craft that would take them home. They needed to lighten the lunar module, which they had burdened with forty pounds of lunar rocks and soil. The pee-bags joined grander detritus like a gold olive branch, a US flag and a commemorative plaque declaring that the men who had left all this mess were peace-loving folk from Earth.

The urine storage bags lie there today, perfectly preserved in lunar dust until some future space tourist grabs them to sell on eBay. Indeed worries about that kind of pilfering have prompted calls for Tranquillity Base to be turned into a sort of Out-of-World Heritage Site, although U.S. lawyers have dampened the ardour of campaigners by advising that this could be interpreted as an American land-grab.

However, nothing daunted, New Mexico State University has stepped into the breach. In a quixotic move it has added Tranquillity Base to an official list of the state's archaeological sites. This means that a bit of the moon is now *de facto* part of New Mexico, which is a sobering thought. Naturally that includes the urine-bags.

Truckers

DRIVING AN EIGHTEEN-WHEEL truck on a tight schedule makes for problems when you need an urgent stop. Truckers in America say it's not uncommon to go for over a hundred miles without finding anywhere lawful to pull over. Which is why so many of them urinate into a plastic juice or milk container and chuck it out of the window as they speed along.

U.S. highways are littered with them. Authorities in the state of Washington reported finding more than a thousand in a hundred-mile stretch of highway in one month, and maintenance crews in Utah pick up 20,000 a year. Several states have passed laws subjecting offenders to fines of up to $1,000 each, although Dakota – wisely perhaps – decided not to post signs warning about the penalties in case it hurt its image.

But this is not merely an American phenomenon, or one unique to truckers. The number of makeshift urine bottles discarded by car-drivers in Europe has grown to such an extent that 'personal disposable urinal bags' are now marketed for use in traffic jams. The TravelJohn disposable urinal, boasting a substance that turns liquid to gel within seconds, offers itself as a handy glove-box accessory for travellers who find themselves gridlocked on a motorway with no loo. This is reported to be a major source of anguish for some motorists.

It's certainly safer than chucking a plastic container filled with urine out of the car window, as the truckers are wont to do. In the summer heat they can build up pressure and have been known to explode when touched. People call them 'trucker bombs'.

UK Biobank

DOCTORS IN CHARGE of storing millions of urine samples in the UK Biobank are rubbing their hands. The prospect of horrible illnesses emerging in high volumes has prompted hope of at last getting to the real causes of many diseases once and for all. Then they will only need to figure out how to cure them.

Half a million people over forty have volunteered to let their urine tell the story of their health from 2007 until they reach the age of seventy. With the average 69-year-old likely to have symptoms of at least three diseases, doctors reckon they will have access to an unprecedented narrative of how conditions like cancer, heart problems, diabetes, arthritis and dementia start to emerge.

Chemicals in the urine will identify what food and drink people have consumed, what medications they are on and how their bodies have dealt with them. Then, when a volunteer next reports any medical problem, the Biobank team will be able to pull out their urine and blood specimens and start determining why the disease has begun.

For the time being doctors just have to keep those urine samples coming. And then wait. They might yet prove to be the most valuable bank deposits in history.

Ulysses

YOU WISH YOU could forget it but you really can't help remembering the way James Joyce describes Leopold Bloom's taste for the inner organs of beasts and fowls: 'Most of all he liked grilled mutton kidneys which gave to his palate a fine tang of faintly scented urine.' There are those of us who have never been able to face a kidney again.

Elsewhere in Joyce's monumental 1922 novel about a Homeric day in the life of Bloom, urine takes its place among hearty descriptions of all kinds of bodily functions and excretions.

One episode, said to have been Joyce's favourite, occurs towards the end of Bloom's Dublin day. He and Stephen Dedalus urinate alongside one another beside the sleeping dog in his back yard. Critics say the urine here is meant to remind us of sacramental wine, and the episode certainly reads like a religious catechism. But you can never be sure with Joyce. He boasted he had put into *Ulysses* 'so many enigmas and puzzles that it will keep the professors busy for centuries'.

The Irish writer was fond of urinary puns*. His first publication, in 1907, was a collection of minor poems that he named after the sound of urine tinkling into a prostitute's pot. The title was *Chamber Music*.

Undulating Paris

AS THE HOME of the open-air pissoir**, France used to be comfortable with the idea of urinating in public. No longer. The mayor of Paris has put his foot down.

For Bertrand Delanoë the old and fast-disappearing *vespasiennes**** were one thing, but peeing on road signs, lamp-posts, the metro and even the walls of the town hall was taking the penchant too far. With around 56,000 square meters of urine-splashed surfaces being

---

See: **Words to the Wise, Loo***
    Clochemerle**
    Vespasian***

cleaned every month in Paris, rising to 65,000 in summer, the mayor decided it was time to act.

In October 2007 he introduced his *pièce de resistance*: an undulating wall built on to the side of vulnerable buildings and designed to ricochet the Frenchman's *pipi* right back in his face.

'It's a case of *l'arroseur arrosé*,'[34] explained Etienne Vanderpooten, a municipal architect who had been working on the problem for more than twenty-five years. 'The jet of pee is rather oblique. If it meets a sloping surface it is sent back to the trousers.'

The mayor can already claim some success in weaning Parisian men off public urination. When he started allowing free entry to the private, self-cleaning sanisettes that are replacing the old pissoirs, usage shot up. Whether the undulating *mur anti-pipi* will prove as effective a deterrent to an entrenched French custom remains to be seen.

Urine Bomb

URINE BOMBS ARE fatally easy to make, as Middle East terror groups and the American CIA have both shown. Nitric acid and urea combine to make urea nitrate. The first ingredient is a readily accessible chemical used in fertilisers; the second is available at the slide of a zip.

Improvised explosive devices used in Israel and Iraq, though not Afghanistan, have frequently been made with urea nitrate. The main explosive in the 1993 bombing of the World Trade Centre in New York comprised 1,200 pounds of it. This bomb failed to bring down the Twin Towers as intended, but it killed six people and injured a thousand, creating a crater 150-feet in diameter that blew a hole five floors deep in the parking garage. Six men, led by a Kuwaiti with links to Al Quaeda, were sentenced to life imprisonment.

Although the World Trade Centre bombing more or less marked the beginning of terrorist use of urine bombs, the American CIA had developed its own bijou version as early as the 1970s. Alarmingly simple instructions on how to prepare their 'piss bomb' are given in a secret Black Book on improvised munitions, allegedly obtained by a weaponry specialist turned reporter.[35] You take ten cups of human or animal urine, boil it down to one cup and mix with nitric acid. The result: one urine bomb.

Another CIA assassination manual of the time, quoted by the same reporter, is a pamphlet called *How to Kill*, which describes how to turn a urinal into a death trap. An electrified grid is wired up to the basin by means of a hidden insulated cord. 'The subject's urine, which is a salty liquid and a perfect conductor of electricity, makes contact with the charged grid, and the shock will kill him,' the author notes briskly.

Uroscopy

MEDIEVAL DOCTORS HAD the barest understanding of internal anatomy. They knew nothing about bacteria, or electricity, or the circulation of the blood. They had no instruments to explore the workings of the body. But what they did have was urine. And in urine they reckoned they had the key to unlock the universe.

The ancient practice of inspecting urine, known as uroscopy, provided evidence of a divinely ordained system that connected man to both the earth and the heavens. It gave medieval thinkers answers to everything and the armour of intellectual certainty. All a physician had to do was interpret a urine sample.

From the seventh century to the Renaissance, uroscopy was propagated as a full-blown science in every medical textbook available to the Western world. Lengthy and complicated treatises were translated back and forwards between Greek and Arabic, Latin and Hebrew. The most awesome achievement was Giles de Corbeil's translation of the influential *De Urinis* – a compilation of sayings of Hippocrates and Galen on the subject – into a 352-line Latin poem. This gave professors across Europe a kind of 'Uroscopy for Beginners' to use in their lectures. Eventually the vernacular tongues of Europe received their own versions.

The Canadian medievalist Ruth Harvey believes that urine, part of 'a system of beautiful coherence', was like the holy grail to the medieval mind. It provided a Theory of Everything.

'Science, philosophy and religion met in their conception of a universe made up of a stationary world composed of the elements of earth, water, air and fire. Man, as the most elaborate creation in the world, reflects the whole composition within himself: he is the microcosm of the universe. The elements inside him have to be in balance for him to be healthy. Urine is the most informative messenger of what is going on.'

The system focussed on the twenty different colours that had been identified in urine, from milky grey through dark green to some rather desperate shades of browny purple[*]. When a medieval physician held a bladder-shaped flask to the light in his right hand, shading it carefully with his left[**], he was initiating a rigorous medical process backed by rational, if misguided, theories going back centuries.   What the colour essentially told the physician was the state of the patient's digestive processes. 'They believed the stomach was set above the liver like a cauldron over a fire,' says Professor Harvey, 'and the food was cooked there until it was turned into blood. The liver was in charge of the process, but if it failed to cook the food sufficiently or overdid the process and burned it, all sorts of dire internal consequences ensued. The patient's urine faithfully reported on all of them.' Pale urine indicated undercooking (diabetes, known as 'the pissing evil', was an example), while the darker ones suggested overcooking. Bright gold urine meant the food was just right.

The medieval theory of gravity also came into play. It was believed the action of the four elements in the body were reproduced in the urine, with the lighter elements – fire and air – rising up, while the heavier ones – earth and water – would sink. So bubbles, foam or oil floating to the surface of the flask would reflect the state of a patient's head, while gravel or sand on the bottom would signal trouble in the kidneys or gout or arthritis in the feet. In the end the Renaissance, ushering in dissection of bodies, discoveries about the circulation of blood and complex wonders revealed by the new microscope, put paid to uroscopy as

---

See: Yellow[*]
     Jordan[**]

a complete science and the four elements faded away. Urine analysis itself degenerated into quackery[*].

But even as late as the beginning of the seventeenth century Shakespeare, in the agonising of Macbeth, was still using it as a metaphor:

If thou could, doctor, cast
The water of my land, find her disease,
And purge it to a sound and pristine health,
I would applaud thee to the very echo,
That should applaud again.

See: Pisse-Prophets[*]

Verdigris

IT'S SUCH A lovely word, *verdigris*, evoking (literally) the greens of Greece, the almost turquoise sheen on weathered copper, the vibrant hues of an old Flemish painting. It's the name given to the bright, bluish-green patina formed on copper, bronze or brass by atmospheric oxidation, a process that happens naturally but is hastened by urine.

The German monk Theophilus called the colour 'Spanish green' and suggested around 1125 that the way to make it was by laying thin copper plates moistened with hot vinegar in a small wooden cask and soaking them in urine.

Ancient Greek artists used verdigris as a pigment, hence the French *vert de Grèce*, while Eadfrith of Lindisfarne illuminated his gorgeous manuscript with it[*]. And in the fifteenth century the Flemish Jan de Eyck was just one of the artists enlivening his paintings with its vivid greens.

The sixteenth-century Italian metallurgist Vannoccio Biringuccio, who was at various times in charge of an iron works

---

See: **Lindisfarne Gospels**[*]

near Sienna, casting cannons for Venice and Florence and running the Pope's foundry in Rome, had a secret tip for using verdigris to improve the yellow colour of silver that contained gold. He advised smearing the silver with verdigris and *sal ammoniac* tempered with urine or vinegar, then heating it over charcoal. Finally he reckoned it should be thrown in more urine and scaled.

Today some furniture restorers still recommend immersing brass or bronze in warm urine to produce a fine aged appearance within the hour. Horse urine is supposed to be especially good. But beware of overdoing it. As Picasso discovered to his cost, beautiful verdigris will lose her looks if she ages too fast[*].

Vespasian

POLITICIANS ARE ALWAYS on the lookout for fresh revenue streams, but one Roman emperor really plumbed the depths of opportunism with a tax on urine.

When he launched the Flavius family dynasty in AD 69, Vespasian had an ambitious construction programme to fund and the damaged finances of the Roman Empire to put in order. Money was tight. But even his son Titus was shocked when he levied a tax on the public urine collected by fullers for use in commercial laundries[**].

Titus duly complained, but Vespasian, famously careful with money, was unabashed. As his biographer Suetonius reports, the emperor thrust a coin from the first payment under his heir's nose and asked pointedly whether he found the smell offensive. Titus conceded that he did not. 'Yet,' retorted his father, 'it comes from urine.'[36]

In the version recounted by another Roman historian, Dio Cassius, Vespasian makes his point with the pithy phrase *Non olet* (literally 'It doesn't smell'), an axiom still heard today in support of the dubious principle that money is money, regardless of where it comes from. F. Scott Fitzgerald may have had it in mind in his

---

See: 𝔓icasso[*]
         𝔯omans[**]

novel *The Great Gatsby*, in which the city of New York is described as rising up across the East River 'in white heaps and sugar lumps all built with a wish out of non-olfactory money'.

Vespasian was by all accounts a pragmatic chap. He had simple tastes (in his early days as emperor he caused a stir by taking his own boots off) and a dry wit that bequeathed us one of the great deathbed pronouncements: 'Damn. I'm already becoming a god.'

But he would surely have been mortified to know how his name is commemorated today: not in the shining feat of Roman architecture he commissioned which we know as the Colosseum, but in the public urinals that are still called *vespasiennes* in France and *vespasiani* in Italy.

Even the good-humoured Vespasian might be pushed to see that joke.

Virgin Mary

MANY ANCIENT CHURCHES struggle with bat urine. The stench from the belfry and the sight of Bibles dripping with pee has prompted irritated vicars to campaign for changes to bat conservation laws. But perhaps the endangered creature deserves all the legal protection it can get, thanks to its sterling work over the centuries in sustaining belief in miracles.

Italians are fond of a story about a statue of the Virgin Mary whose copious weeping was a source of wonder to medieval worshippers. Pilgrims flocked to thrill at the sight. In more sceptical times the tears staining her face were revealed to be bat urine.

In another continental cathedral spots of martyr's blood were reputed to appear on the flagstones each morning, a considerable comfort to the pious until a travelling Victorian clergyman visited. Rev. William Buckland was a future dean of Westminster with an enthusiasm for putting bizarre things in his mouth (he ate leopards, crocodiles, dormice and part of the heart of Louis IV). A drop of martyr's blood was just the sort of challenge he relished. Kneeling on the flagstones, he leant forward and hazarded a discreet lick. 'Bat's urine,' he pronounced at once, doubtless with a smack of the lips.

Mr Buckland died in an insane asylum in 1856.

Vitalism

THE BRILLIANT YOUNG chemist could hardly contain his excitement when he put pen to paper in 1828 to report that he had discovered how to isolate an important organic compound found in urine *without* urine. 'I must tell you that I can make urea without needing a kidney, either man or dog,' he whooped to his friend Jöns Jacob Berzelius.

The discovery was philosophical as well as scientific dynamite. By proving for the first time that an organic compound could be made artificially, Friedrich Wöhler fatally undermined long-established ideas about the mysterious vital spirit thought to animate human life.

Wöhler stumbled on urea accidentally, in the process of trying to prepare ammonium cyanate. When he wrote to his mentor Berzelius in Stockholm, he was bursting with the news. 'I can no longer, so to speak, hold my chemical water,' he burbled. 'The ammonium salt of cyanic acid is urea.'

Urea had first been discovered by the French pharmacist Hilarie Rouelle in 1773 when he boiled urine dry. It was named *urée* in 1799 by another pair of French chemists, one of whom, Antoine Fourcroy, noted that the examination of urine had 'furnished the most singular discoveries to chemistry'.

In 1812 a British doctor and amateur chemist, John Davy, synthesized a substance from ammonia and phosgene, but only later was this understood to be urea. So it fell to the Swedish-trained, German chemist Wöhler to make history, not only by synthesising urea and recognising it as such, but also by blowing a hole through the notion that organic and inorganic compounds were different kinds of matter.

The quasi-religious theory of Vitalism, which held sway in various forms from the seventeenth to the nineteenth centuries, was a reaction to purely mechanistic explanations of the universe. Living material, it was believed, was animated by some sort of mysterious 'life-force' which set it apart from other kinds of matter. But by managing a process in his laboratory that scientists had thought could only be done within a living organism, Wöhler showed that the body's chemical reactions followed the laws of nature in exactly the same way as chemical reactions anywhere else.

Synthetic urea went on to become the wonder compound used today in fertilizers, cosmetics, plastics, animal feed, glues, toilet bowl cleaners, dish-washing detergents, hair-colouring products, pesticides, fungicides and skin moisturizers[*]. Wöhler went on to isolate several other chemical elements. But he was always aware that urea, the big one, had shaken the foundations of much more than chemistry. As he wrote to Berzelius, he had witnessed 'the great tragedy of science, the slaying of a beautiful hypothesis by an ugly fact'.

_____

See: Skin[*]

Warhol

WHEN ANDY WARHOL was preparing his so-called 'oxidation paintings', he always led visitors into his New York studio with an extra bounce. Wittingly or not, they were about to become suppliers of one of his main ingredients. Once inside the studio, they were expected to give generously to the strangely beautiful work created by urine on copper metallic-painted canvas.

Warhol's biographer, Bob Colacello, described the friends who helped America's celebrated pop artist to oxidise the copper paint as 'ghost-pissers'. He said Warhol was particularly gratified by his friend Ronnie Cutrone's contribution. Cutrone was instructed not to pee when he got up in the morning but to hold it in until he reached the studio. His predilection for Vitamin B apparently turned the copper a particularly fetching shade of green.

The canvasses had an entirely different feel from the pop images that made Warhol famous. These were iridescent, offering a sensuous enjoyment of the paint, full of richly coloured strokes and drips in coppery yellow, green and orange. Reviewing the New York exhibition of the Oxidation Series in 1986, Grace Glueck described them as 'random, perverse creations, yet they are seriously beautiful'.

No-one was ever sure what Warhol intended the act of urination to symbolise, if anything. Perhaps it was just the oxidation process itself that interested him. Urine had been used for centuries to speed up the patination of bronze sculptures, not least by Pablo Picasso[*].

Warhol was not always in a hurry to admit to the technique. He said once of the oxidation paintings: 'These nice older women were asking me how I'd done them and I didn't have the heart to tell them what they really were, because their noses were right up against them.'

Wee Chefs

ON EARTH AND off it, there's nothing like urine to spice up a meal when water is too precious to waste or too heavy to carry. U.S. troops use it to rehydrate dried food in emergencies and NASA, always on the lookout for space innovations, have found a novel way of cooking with it.

The army finds that rehydrating dried rations with a quick pee can reduce the amount soldiers need to carry: a full 7lbs a day of the 8lb food load can be saved. The meals come in special plastic pouches with filters strong enough to screen out toxins and bacteria, which means they can be rehydrated by any liquid that comes to hand in the field, including muddy swamp water. Troops tend to find nothing comes to hand quite as easily as urine, which is pretty clean anyway.

NASA is meanwhile making urine into water that can be added to normal food in space. It's part of a $250 million regenerative life support system, designed to enable astronauts to travel further into space with fewer drop-offs from visiting spacecraft.

The U.S. space agency has developed a contraption that uses distillation, filtration, oxidation and ionisation to turn a crew's urine and sweat, along with moisture from the air, into drinking water. The final step is to add iodine to control microbial growth. After the system is up and running, the plan is to use the water to cook

See: 𝔓icasso[*]

meals on board the spacecraft, which astronauts have always said could do with some pepping up.

'Other than a faint taste of iodine, it's just as refreshing as any other kind of water,' said NASA's Bob Bagdigian, the system's lead engineer, reassuringly. 'I've got some in my fridge.'

Wheelie Bins

WITH PUBLIC CONVENIENCES in terminal decline and more and more revellers too drunk to find one anyway, Britain's towns are desperate for a solution to pee-soaked streets. How about a bin that doubles as a urinal?

Swiss designer Stephan Bischoff has developed a plastic wheelie bin with an extra compartment down the back for peeing into. This funnels the urine into a removable compost tray in the base to be converted into bio-fertiliser. You can even open the lid to pop your rubbish in at the top as usual. Stamped with a council logo on one side, the bin looks appealingly normal.

Mr Bischoff tried out the wheelie bin in south London (a better bet for testing his prototype, one imagines, than anywhere in pin-clean Switzerland) and is hoping to persuade councils in Britain to take it on.

He should try thirsty Glasgow where, as in many cities, public urination has been on the increase. Strathclyde police recorded a doubling of offences in five years across their patch, which includes the city itself, from 2,595 to 4,566 a year. Most offenders were slapped with £40 fixed penalty fines.

Whether the presence of Stephan's wheelie would deter that sort of drink-fuelled offender is debateable. The bin is unlikely to attract the growing minority of hard-drinking girls who also swell the statistics. But as public toilets up and down the country continue to close – thousands have gone in the last decade because of high maintenance costs – wheelie bin urinals might just catch on with the blokes.

Whizzinator

AMONG THE MANY products designed to thwart the world's drug testers, one invention stands out. For sheer ingenuity, cheek and aplomb, the Whizzinator reigns supreme.

It's a prosthetic penis, which was discovered in the luggage of the American footballer Onterrio Smith in 2005, when the Minnesota Vikings player was stopped on his way through Minneapolis-St Paul International Airport. Vials of white powder were also found in his luggage.

The Whizzinator works by attaching to a bag that emits reconstituted urine from freeze-dried crystals, in the hope of fooling the beady-eyed official charged with observing an athlete's urine sample collection[*]. It comes in five fetching flesh tones to suit different ethnic groups and the components fit neatly inside a jock strap. No-one knows how many testers the Whizzinator might already have slipped past[**] before airport officials impounded it.

Onterrio Smith told police he was taking the kit to his cousin.

Woad

WOAD PRODUCED A dye so easily made with urine that even peasants owned blue garments, so indelible that it is still the only colour not to have faded from the Bayeux Tapestry and so foul-smelling that Elizabeth I banned its production anywhere near her. With its towering yellow blossom, the native European woad plant was the principal dyestuff of the medieval world.

It's no surprise that the reek of large-scale woad production offended the royal nose. To instigate production of the blue indigotin pigment, the leaves were crushed, dried, formed into small woad balls and then left to ferment for long periods in barrels of urine. That was smelly enough. But once the dyeing began, the woad vat gave off another noxious odour caused by dimethyl disulphide and methanethiol (seriously smelly chemicals associated with the

---

See: Chaperone[*]
     Sport[**]

anaerobic microbial breakdown of plants). You can understand why Queen Elizabeth put her foot down.

Elizabeth decreed that no woad processing should be allowed within several miles of her royal residences, until someone could figure out a way of mitigating the smell. Or, as she put it, 'until there may be a further consideration had how the same may be suffered with some toleration'. She also ordered that during any travels through the country, she 'might not be driven out of the towns by the woade infecting the air near them'.

However, as the emperor Vespasian wryly observed, urine may smell but money does not*. Woad was a vital cash crop across Europe, generating big profits and plentiful labour. In England it was claimed that forty acres would keep 160 people, mainly women and children, in work for a third of the year.

In fact, its cultivation in England grew so fast during the sixteenth century that woad was beginning to threaten cereal production and animal grazing.

That gave Elizabeth a more public-spirited excuse for controlling its production. With food shortages looming in 1585, she issued a *Proclamation Against The Sowing of Woade* to prevent too much fertile land being devoted to the dye-plant. Regulations were amended in 1587 to allow no more than forty or sixty acres of woad in any one parish and no more than twenty acres sown by one person a year.

Woad dye had a unique colour-fast quality, which is why of the three primary colours illustrating the story of the Norman Conquest in the Bayeux Tapestry (red from madder roots, yellow from mignonette and blue from woad), it is the blue which best survives. In Coventry, a centre of the medieval wool trade, woad's reputation for not fading after washing gave rise to the phrase 'as true as Coventry blue'. According to the naturalist John Ray in 1670, this was 'to signifie one that was always the same and like himself'.[37]

A woad-based pigment was also used for the stunning blue

See: Vespasian*

colours in the illuminated seventh-century Lindisfarne Gospels[*]
and, long before that, on the faces of the warrior queen Boudicca
and her Iceni tribesmen[**].

Woad remained the dominant blue dye across Europe until a
deeper, richer rival from Asia, also prepared with urine, began to
supplant it[***]. Although woad producers, rallying as so-called
Woadites, put pressure on the governments of England, France and
Germany to ban the import of the upstart indigo, mass woad
production was waning by the late seventeenth century. Right up
to the 1930s, however, it was specially grown in Lincolnshire to
provide a colour-fast dye to keep the police, military and naval
uniforms of the boys in blue from fading.

See: Lindisfarne Gospels[*]
     Queen Boudicca[**]
     Indigo[***]

Xanthippe

XANTHIPPE WAS THE reputedly shrewish second wife of the classical Greek philosopher Socrates. Her reputation as the harridan from hell was sealed by Geoffrey Chaucer in his fourteenth-century masterpiece *The Canterbury Tales*, in which the Wife of Bath recounts in her faux-learned and comically misogynistic prologue the 'sorrow and woe' that Xanthippe caused her husband by hurling urine over his head. The attack is received by Socrates, she suggests, with the resigned wit of a man who has learned not to protest at wifely excesses. The Wife of Bath describes:

> How Xantippa caste pisse upon his heed.
> This sely man sat stille as he were deed;
> He wipte his heed, namoore dorste he seyn,
> But 'Er that thonder stynte, comth a reyn!'[38]

Chaucer was not the first to put the boot into Xanthippe, whose name in Greek, Blonde Horse, is prettier than her reputation. Xenophon, a contemporary of her husband, said Socrates himself had agreed with a suggestion that the mother of his three sons was 'the hardest to get along with of all the women there are'. Socrates had even compared her to a spirited horse, on the somewhat unconvincing grounds that if he could tolerate this woman, he could certainly manage anyone else.

Xanthippe was considerably younger than her husband and she did have her defenders. Socrates' own student Plato suggested she was nothing less than a devoted wife and mother, while the early fifteenth-century writer Christin de Pisan argued in *The Book of the City of Ladies* that Xanthippe had in fact been a good woman, possessed of great learning. But it was all to no avail. After Chaucer the reputation of Socrates' wife would always rest on a pot of piss.

𝔛-𝔯𝔞𝔱𝔢𝔡

WHEN ROCK AND roll's sharpest social critic Frank Zappa released 'Bobby Brown (Goes Down)' on his *Sheik Yerbouti* album in 1979, Europeans loved the song and the United States promptly banned it. With lyrics like 'I can take about an hour on the tower of power / 'Long as I gets a little golden shower', nobody was very surprised. Censors get twitchy about urolagnia.

The word is from the Greek *ouron* (urine) and *lagneia* (lust), which would seem to cover the main bases. However people who get sexual pleasure from urinating on others, or being urinated on by them, usually prefer the 'golden shower' euphemism. In New Zealand you can go to prison for promoting the practice in print or film, so for readers in Wellington we have to be circumspect.

Frank Zappa's song is as mockingly satirical as most of his work. Bobby Brown's lurid sexual encounters are peppered with the ironic refrain 'Oh God, I am the American dream' – a frequent target for the droopy-moustachioed Zappa. But it's probably no surprise that the song did best in continental Europe, where rock fans unfamiliar with English idioms may have had less of a clue about what he was on about. Its huge popularity there helped *Sheik Yerbouti* to become the best-selling album of Zappa's thirty-year career.

The fiercely intelligent Zappa, lead guitarist of the Mothers of Invention and the most prolific cross-genre composer of his age, is fondly remembered for his description of rock journalists as 'people who can't write, interviewing people who can't talk, for people who can't read'. If anyone deserved to get away with a lyrical golden shower, it was him.

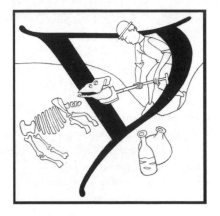

Yaddlethorpe

IN 1856 A man digging in his garden in the village of Yaddlethorpe in Lincolnshire unearthed the skeleton of a horse or an ox. Near to it lay two bottles containing pins, needles, human hair and a stinking fluid reckoned to be urine. They were the long-buried weapons of credulous folk against people imagined to be witches.

It was believed you could free yourself of a spell by magically stopping the guilty witch's ability to urinate. A person thought to be the victim of witchcraft would bottle up his or her own urine along with iron nails, needles and some hair and fingernail parings – then wait for it to effect physical torment on the unhappy soul deemed to have caused the upset.

In 1681 an English vicar, Joseph Glanvill, produced a collection of folklore so confidently affirming the malign power of witchcraft that it influenced the notorious Salem witch trials in Massachusetts eleven years later.[38] He told the story of a man who put his ailing wife's urine into a bottle with pins and needles and nails, corked them up and warmed the bottle on the fire. Unfortunately, Glanvill tells us, 'the cork bounced out, and the urine, pins, nails and needles all flew up ... and his wife continued in the same trouble and languishment still'.

The husband was then advised to follow the same procedure again but this time to bury the bottle in the ground. This the man did. His wife began to mend and was soon 'finely well recovered'.

Then the twist in the tale: 'But there came a woman from a town some miles off to their house, with a lamentable out-cry, that they had killed her husband. [That] husband was a wizzard and had bewitched this mans wife.' Which, as far as Glanvill was concerned, proved everything.

Animals subject to misfortune or prone to stroppy behaviour received the same treatment, as the Yaddlethorpe discovery attests. The English antiquary John Aubrey, who was fascinated by reports of supernatural phenomena, related in his 1696 *Miscellanies*: 'Mr Sp. told me that his horse was bewitched, would break bridles and strong halters, like a Samson. They filled a bottle of the horse's urine, stopped it with a cork ... and then buried it under ground: and the party suspected to be the witch fell ill, that he could not make water, of which he died.'[39]

Even when bottling urine was not involved, the aim was still to make the witch suffer the agonies of being unable to urinate and by that means flush him or her into the open. A farmer near Torrington, whose calves were stillborn, was advised to hang a calf over the fire on the chimney crook and then sneak into the putative witch's house, catch three fleas from her bed and cork them inside a bottle. As long as these fleas were stuck in the bottle, the witch would never be able to urinate. After four or five days, the farmer was assured, she would be driven to pass his window and look in – at which point the spell would be broken.

The world's most complete 'witch bottle' was unearthed in the Greenwich area of London. CT scans and chemical analysis revealed the contents to include human urine, brimstone, twelve iron nails, eight brass pins, hair, possible navel fluff, a piece of heart-shaped leather pierced by a bent nail, and ten fingernail clippings. Archaeologists were even able to tell that the benighted soul who collected all this was a smoker: the urine still had nicotine in it.

Cruel in intention as the practice was, for anyone suspected of being a witch those imaginary urinary torments would have been a considerably better bet than drowning. Or than the hangings that awaited the fourteen women and five men convicted of witchcraft at Salem.

Yeast

IN ONE OF the unspeakably brutal internment camps in Dutch Indonesia during the Second World War, inmates were appalled to hear that bread was suddenly off the menu: the Japanese had suspended yeast supplies. Since dry bread was all they ever got for lunch, this was a hammer blow. But the internees found a solution in the end, in a substance that had played an unheralded role in bread-making for centuries.

Pieter Wiederhold, the young son of a Dutch factory manager in Java, was among those who had been interned with his family when Japanese troops swept through Indonesia after the bombing of Pearl Harbour, seizing property and imprisoning citizens. Wiederhold witnessed disease, malnutrition, torture and death in the prison camps. The ban on yeast threatened more privation.

However, among the internees in this camp were trained chemists. What, they wondered, could be used instead of yeast? After some trial and error, a message went round the camp requesting everyone to urinate from now on into a number of strategically placed large drums. These were collected twice daily and carted off to the camp kitchen.

There, recalled Wiederhold, who emigrated later to the United States, the urine was boiled up and used to give them bread again. 'We ate that kind of bread for the next two years,' he said.

In fact, those prison camp chemists were tapping into a long tradition that had also served brewers well[*]. In the 1950s an elderly woman in rural Galway in Ireland could still remember urine being collected, allowed to go stale in a loosely covered vessel and then used for bread-making. For people adept at putting everything to good use, it proved an ideal substitute for yeast in lightening and softening the dough.

See: Beer[*]

The secret is ammonium carbonate, formed when the urea in stale urine combines with water. It can be distilled, as the Dutch internees found, in a simple cooking pot. Ammonium carbonate decomposes to form ammonia and carbon dioxide, and it's these gases that cause the pockets or bubbles of air that make the dough rise. When the dough is then baked, the air pockets set, giving the bread its soft and spongy texture.

Eventually the advent of baking soda – sodium bicarbonate put paid to the need for ammonium carbonate to leaven dough. But synthetically produced 'baker's ammonia' is still a popular leavening agent in northern Europe and Scandinavia. Connoisseurs there say baking soda doesn't leave the finished product nearly so light and airy.

Pieter Wiederhold said nothing about whether the bread in his Indonesian camp was light and airy, or how the flavour compared with other kinds. No doubt he didn't care. However the bread tasted, he and his fellow internees had reason to be grateful to the urine that made it rise again.

Yeats

WHEN IRELAND'S W.B. Yeats and Scotland's Hugh MacDiarmid wandered through Dublin together in August 1928, the empty night streets witnessed two of the twentieth century's finest wordsmiths sealing their friendship with a 'crossed swords' pee.

Yeats was 63. The poet who had lamented the 'terrible beauty' of the Easter Rising and brilliantly nailed the spirit of the age ('The best lack all conviction, while the worst / Are full of passionate intensity') was already recognised as a towering literary figure. MacDiarmid, just 36, had recently established himself as the principal figure in modern Scottish letters with the scintillatingly inventive 'A Drunk Man Looks at the Thistle'.

MacDiarmid was on a visit to Dublin, and the pair met at the poet George Russell's house before sauntering home together. 'I will never forget the privilege and pleasure I enjoyed as we walked back – he to Fitzwilliam Square and I to Ely Place – in the *wee sma' 'oors* of the following morning,' MacDiarmid recalled later.

They had not been boozing. Much to the Scottish poet's horror, the evening had been fuelled by nothing more than natural lemonade. But Yeats had downed enough to announce, as they wandered the deserted streets of Dublin, 'Well, if you'll excuse me, I must urinate', which he promptly did in the middle of the road. MacDiarmid lost no time in joining him.

'I thought to myself, well, what an Irish senator can do there's no reason why a Scottish magistrate can't, so I crossed swords with him and we became very friendly after that.'

Neither poet was ever a man to pass up an opportunity for symbolism.

Yellow

URINE GETS ITS colour from clapped-out red blood cells. They die after about 120 days and are processed by the liver to leave a yellow pigment called urochrome. This passes into the bloodstream and is filtered out by the kidneys, leaving that yellowish hue we all know so well.

But yellow is not an inevitable fixture. Health, diet and drug intake can alter the colour spectacularly, as physicians have been observing for a very long time. Fragments of tablets in the British Museum reveal that the Babylonians were paying close attention to different shades and consistency four thousand years before the birth of Christ. These are described as 'white or pure', 'black or dark', formed 'like clouds', 'bright red' or, alarmingly, 'very bright red'. Ancient Sanskrit works of medicine came up with even more telling images, such as 'floury white', or the colour of brandy or honey.

In medieval manuscripts the hues of urine evoke a world of exotic colour and unsettling beauty. They have strange Greek names like *carapos*, the colour of a camel's hair – which must have puzzled the less well-travelled practitioners. In *The Book of the Deeming of Urine* (1378) the Dominican monk and energetic horticulturalist Henry Daniel hazarded that camel-coloured urine was 'a joyous colour signifying good health'. He also noted that men's urine was usually brighter than women's and a 'livid' shade was a sign of lung disease.

The vibrant colours of unhealthy urine make early textbooks startlingly vivid. Turning the pages of a fourteenth-century quasi-alchemical work like the *Judicium Urinarum*[40], in which ill health is depicted in a lurid rainbow of hand-painted urine flasks, can leave you feeling decidedly seedy yourself.

Medieval physicians identified twenty colours as a guide to diagnosis[*]. A modern, equally hit-or-miss ready-reckoner might include:

* **Almost colourless:** you've been drinking a lot of water.
* **Very dark and concentrated:** a sign of dehydration.
* **Blue:** a possible inherited tendency to high levels of calcium, or perhaps something catastrophically worse[**].
* **Red:** blood may be present (possibly from a bladder infection) or it's porphyria[***]. More likely you've had beetroot for dinner[****].
* **Dark yellow:** a liver disorder or jaundice.
* **Bright orange:** too many carrots or Vitamin C.
* **Spring green:** too much Vitamin B[*****].
* **Emerald green:** a urinary tract infection, bile pigment or certain drugs.
* **Brown, smoky or black:** hepatitis, copper poisoning or too many fava beans.

Yeti

ONCE YETIS MERELY teased mountaineers with large footprints in the snow or the odd giant hand misplaced in a Buddhist monastery. Now they are getting careless. Traces of supposed yeti urine have been found as far apart as China and the Himalayas. Strangely, it is said to look similar to any other animal's pee. There's just more of it.

See: 𝔘roscopy[*]
    𝔊eorge III[**]
    𝔊eorge III[***]
    𝔅eeting the 𝔊olour[****]
    𝔚arhol[*****]

China's species of yeti, known as the *yeren* (wildman) was spotted in the forested mountains of Hubei province in 2003, where there have been scores of reported sightings over the centuries. Shang Zhengmin, a reporter for a local radio station, was in a jeep with five locals in the Shennongjia Nature Reserve when they turned a corner and saw a 'grey creature' moving quickly away from the road.

They reported that the thing was about 5ft 5in tall with a crooked back and shoulder-length black hair. It had left footprints 12 inches long, which is big for a little fellow. But the real surprise was the patch of 'foul-smelling, urine-like liquid' which stretched for an incredible ten feet. This must have been some pee. By the time the jeep had stopped, the animal had inconveniently disappeared.

In 2008 the Spanish mountaineer Jose Ramon Bacelar found urine beside tracks in the Himalayas that he too claimed was evidence of the yeti, a word derived in the 1930s from the Tibetan *yeh-teh* (little manlike animal).

Urine trails are unlikely to advance the truth about yetis much further than any other apparent traces. The skeleton of a supposed yeti hand from the Pangboche monastery in Nepal caused a stir in 1959, when some bone fragments were stolen by the mountaineer Peter Byrne and allegedly flown to London in the luggage of the American actor James Stewart. The bones were examined at London University by primatologist W.C. Osman Hill, who initially concluded that they were hominid and later that they were a closer match with a Neanderthal.

Most experts think the yeti is a bear. With a normal bladder, probably.

Ziggy Stardust

THE ENGLISH MUSICIAN David Bowie has sold around 136 million albums and forged a career out of brilliant musical innovation and personal reinvention. But the singer, famous for his flamboyant *alter ego* Ziggy Stardust, went through periods of being seriously strange – not least when he began keeping his urine, hair and fingernail clippings in the fridge.

It was once believed that by bottling up urine and fingernails you could break a magic spell and bring torment on the witch responsible[*]. Bowie seems to have been trying to protect himself from witchcraft in this age-old manner by bottling his own.

He was living in Los Angeles at the time, preparing his 1976 album *Station to Station*. Nobody knows why he became convinced that the evil forces of black magic were out to get him, particularly in the shape of Jimmy Page, founder of the rock band Led Zeppelin, who had an interest in the occult. But, then, Bowie also believed the Rolling Stones were sending him messages in their record sleeves.

See: 𝔜𝔞𝔡𝔡𝔩𝔢𝔱𝔥𝔬𝔯𝔭𝔢[*]

The singer is said to have admitted in later years that his mind was disordered by cocaine at the time, which goes some way to explaining things. But it still leaves you wondering what happened when he made a grab for something strong to help him unwind after a gig.

300

VISITORS TO EDINBURGH Zoo are unlikely to forget how rhinos mark their territory. In the wild the animals' boundary tends to be a nitrogen-fried line of grassland. But in Edinburgh the scent-marking urge drives the zoo's two adult Indian males straight to the tall fence they share with onlookers clustering on the other side.

The pair potter around their log-piles, sniff a bit and then turn their backs to the fence. How charming, think the watchers. What *are* they doing? The urine jet travels backwards and covers a distance of six to eight feet, so they soon find out. There is a direct hit (or a very near miss) at least once a week in the summer.

The rhinos produce 24 litres of pee each a day, which is going some. They are the most prolific urinators in a zoo that has to deal with around 1,000 litres of the stuff every day from 1,200 animals of all sizes. That doesn't include the mass of white guano left by the raucous inhabitants of the world's largest captive penguin colony. It takes three keepers two hours a day to wash down that enclosure, in which more than 200 gentoos, rockhoppers and king penguins save water by excreting their metabolic waste in the form of intensely smelly uric acid.

But not all of Edinburgh Zoo's urinary output is washed away. Some of it heads for the onsite genetics lab for DNA extraction. With only a tiny amount of DNA in urine, there is new and complex chemistry involved in amplifying this to a point where genetic marking, paternity or species identification can be determined. These forensic processes also contribute to investigations outside the zoo. For crimes like wildlife trafficking or dog-fighting, DNA evidence can be crucial.

A much larger dollop of urine is collected from dung and

hay-beds to accelerate composting for the zoo's nursery. Some of the compost is packaged and then sold on to visitors. With hundreds of thousands of litres to get rid of every year, the more ways a zoo can find to exploit urine commercially, the happier its balance sheet.

In 2009 the hopes of gardeners trying to protect their vegetable patches from neighbourhood cats were raised to fever-pitch by a rumour that Chester Zoo was offering lion and tiger pee for sale. Anxious to pre-empt a flood of importunate vegetable growers, the zoo issued a somewhat brittle plea in *The Guardian*, which announced: 'Chester Zoo would like to forestall requests for its big cats' urine: it asks us to make clear that it does not in fact sell either tiger or lion urine. Many years ago the zoo sold elephant dung, but it no longer does.'

Edinburgh Zoo has not ventured into pee sales either, although tapping into the desperation of gardeners to drive off domestic cats is perhaps a marketing area worth considering. As for rhino urine, visitors are prone to take some home with them whether they want it or not.

Acknowledgements

A voice drifted over from the neighbouring pillow one night at 1.30 a.m. I had just been regaling the prone form beside me with that day's investigations into Joseph Lister's success in growing bacteria-inhibiting mould on his urine – a welcome entry for L. Sixty years before Fleming got the credit for discovering antibiotics, Lister had seen it in his urine flask.

The duvet stirred. 'By the way,' it said, 'I've thought of an entry for X.'

'Wonderful.' X was a problem. 'What is it?'

'X-husband,' grunted the mound, and turned over.

So, undying thanks to Norman, mercifully still hanging in there, who put up with more conversations about pee than a man should have to bear. Also to my sisters, Margaret and Anna, for heroically supporting me with domestic cover and emergency research.

I encountered some compelling companions on my journey into the life of pee. Nicholas Walt inviting me to sniff some of the world's last remaining balls of Indian Yellow. Katie Campbell and Ina Morrison rhapsodising dreamily about the *waulking* over tea and scones on Harris. Keith Rees in Carmarthenshire, proud to show off the last ammonia-stained bucket from an old Welsh *pandy*. Sam Fountain enthusing over the invention that liberates women. Finnbogi Bernódusson waving his arms indignantly on the shore of a sun-caressed fjord as he revealed the secret of Icelandic shark-meat. Physicist Victoria Harris, still bubbling with excitement as she recalled the moment that could transform the lives of refugees. Medievalist Ruth Harvey, so movingly entranced by the beauty of the Theory of Everything.

I am grateful to every one of them – not least because they are all people who managed to say 'urine' without sounding embarrassed or looking anything like as shifty as I did whenever I had to reveal what I was writing. Their stories encouraged me to believe it was possible to celebrate the quirky story of pee without resorting to arch apology or *too* many puns.

Many others responded with warmth and good humour when somewhat startlingly approached out of the blue for their insights on pee. Particular thanks to the School of English at St Andrews University, especially Prof. Robert Crawford (who can claim credit for the title), Dr Michael Herbert and Dr Sara Lodge; scientists James Glover, Dr Chris Cooksey, Dr David Petts, Steve Clarke and Prof. Alan Dronsfield; classicists Dr Mark Bradley of Nottingham University, whose article in the *Journal of Roman Archaeology 15*, 2002, 'It all comes out in the wash: Looking harder at the Roman *fullonica*' was both fascinating and invaluable, and Dr Ralph Anderson at St Andrews; animal expert Iain Valentine at Edinburgh Zoo; and the impressively numerate Aisling Winston of the University of Denver. Thanks also to Mic Calder, Bridget Clifford, Richard Demarco, Adam Goldwater, Chris Gravett, Marta Guðjónsdóttir, Hörður Högnason, Bára Hreiðarsdóttir, Vicki Jack, John Lloyd, John Randall, Steve Turner and Joe Winston.

Finally, heartfelt thanks to my agent Pat Lomax and especially to my brilliant editor Sam Harrison, who understood what I was trying to do and kept me aiming high.

Notes

1 Sidney Oldall Addy, *A Glossary of Words Used in the Neighbourhood of Sheffield*, 1888.

2 Konrad Heresbach, *Foure Bookes of Husbandry*, translated from the German in 1577.

3 James Howell, Proverbs 18, in *Lexicon Tetraglotton*, an English-French-Italian-Spanish dictionary, 1660.

4 Adam Hart-Davis and Emily Troscianko, *Taking the Piss: A Potted History of Pee*, The Chalford Press, 2006, on which I have relied for the details of the trade.

5 World Anti-Doping Program, *Guidelines for Urine Sample Collection*, June 2004.

6 Field Marshall Lord Alanbrooke, *War Diaries 1939-1945*, edited by Alex Danchev and Daniel Todman, Phoenix Press, 2002.

7 'The Croydon Typhoid Inquiry: Mr H. L. Murphy's Report', *The British Medical Journal*, 19 February 1938.

8 Charles H. Duncan, *Autotherapy*, self-published, 1918.

9 Martha M. Christy, *Your Own Perfect Medicine: The Incredible Proven Natural Miracle Cure that Medical Science has Never Revealed!*, Wishland Publishing, 1994.

10 William Partridge, *A Practical Treatise on Dying*, New York, 1834.

11 Charles M Larson, *Numismatic Forgery*, Zyrus Press, 2004.

12 Frederick Chattaway, 'The Action of Chlorine upon Urea Whereby a Dichloro Urea is Produced', *Proceedings of the Royal Society of London*, December 1908.

13 A.C. Johnson *et al*, 'Do cytotoxic chemotherapy drugs discharged into rivers pose a risk to the environment and human health?', *Journal of Hydrology*, 2008

14 Although the report cites UK rivers, Scottish Water says the 2% of drinking water in Scotland that does not come from virgin reservoirs is taken from rivers where there is no recycling: 'We use no recycled water.'

15 Susan Jobling *et al*, 'Statistical Modeling Suggests that Antiandrogens in Effluents from Wastewater Treatment Works Contribute to Widespread Sexual Disruption in Fish Living in English Rivers,' *Environ Health Perspect*, January 2009.

16 Quoted in an essay by Chris Cooksey and Alan T. Dronsfield, 'George III, Indigo and the Blue Ring Test', *Education in Chemistry*, Royal Society of Chemistry, March 2008.

17 *Calendar of State Papers, Domestic Series, of the Reign of Charles I*, 1629 1631, Public Record Office, 1860.

18 He is also famous for articulating Boyle's Law: that the volume of a gas varies inversely to its pressure.

19 Royal Gardens, Kew, 'Indian Yellow', *Bulletin of Miscellaneous Information 39*, March, 1890.

20 Kew Bulletin, *ibid*

21 Victoria Finlay, *Colour: Travels through the Paintbox*, Hodder, 2002,

22 M. Locq '*Mémoire sur la fabrication et l'emploi de l'orseille*', *Annales de Chimie*, Paris, 1812.

23 Eadfrith also made white by crushing Lindisfarne seashells, yellow from the mineral orpiment and the rich reddish orange hues from toasted lead. The ink was from iron salts. The feathers of the

island's ubiquitous geese made his pens.

24 Franklin C. Clark, 'A Brief History of Antiseptic Surgery', *Medical Library and Historical Journal*, September 1907.

25 The inscription reads in German: 'Anno domini 1787 liess Wolfgang Amadeus Mozart auf seiner Reise nach Prag just an dieser Stelle seine Kutsche anhalten. Seither heisst im Volksmund dieser Stein PINKELSTEIN.'

26 'Human Urine in Mud Brick Construction', *Live Project*, Sheffield University, 2007. The report suggests that at just over 1.01 litres a day, a fully nourished refugee would produce 370 litres of urine in a year. A family of four would require 1,950 bricks and 2,933 litres of urine to build a basic mud brick shelter, taking them at least two years.

27 Team member Edward Abraham's laboratory notes describe how 3.7 litres of the patient's urine was combined with one-third volume of the organic solvents chloroform and ether, then extracted into ether and re-extracted into dilute sodium hydroxide solution. Then 550ml of water solution was re-extracted with ether and once again mixed with ether. Again it was extracted with sodium hydroxide solution and finally freeze-dried. The result, after all this labour, was a mere half-gram of impure penicillin.

28 '*Omnes vero se Britanni vitro inficiunt, quod caeruleum efficit colorem, atque hoc horridiores sunt in pugna aspectu.*'

29 *Robin Hood's Garland*, a ballad printed in the eighteenth century.

30 Martial, *Epigrams*, Book 6, V, 93: '*Tam male Thais olet quam non fullonis avari testa vetus media, sed modo fracta via.*'

31 Richard Hutton, *The Stations of the Sun: A History of the Ritual Year in Britain*, Oxford University Press, 1996.

32 Carolyn M. Willis et al, 'Olfactory detection of human bladder cancer by dogs: proof of principle study', *British Medical Journal*, 25 September 2004.

33 Joseph Lemasolai Lekuton and Herman J. Viola, *Facing the Lion: Growing Up Masai on the African Savannah*, National Geographic Books, 2005.

34 '*nunc Celtiber es; Celtiberia in terra, quod quisque minxit, hoc sibi solet mane dentem atque russam defricare gingiuam, ut quo iste uester expolitior dens est, hoc te amplius bibisse praedicet loti*'.

35 'The sprinkler sprinkled.'

36 Andrew Stark (pseudonym), 'The CIA's Secret Weapons Systems', *Gallery*, June 1978.

37 '*Reprehendenti filio Tito, quod etiam urinae vectigal commentus esset, pecuniam ex prima pensione admovit ad nares, sciscitans num odore offenderetur: at illo negante "Atque" inquit "e lotio est.*", Suetonius, *De Vita Caesarum-Divus Vespasianus*, XXIII. 3

38 John Ray, *A Compleat Collection of English Proverbs*, 1670.

39 '*How Xanthippe threw piss upon his head. This hapless man sat still, as he were dead; He wiped his head, no more durst he complain Than "Ere the thunder ceases comes the rain.*"'

40 Joseph Glanvill, *Sadducismus Triumphatus*, 1681.

41 John Aubrey, *Miscellanies*, 1696.

42 The oldest medical manuscript in the library of the Royal College of Physicians, Edinburgh.